Optional Federal Chartering and Regulation of Insurance Companies

Edited by Peter J. Wallison

The AEI Press

Publisher for the American Enterprise Institute
WASHINGTON, D.C.

2000

Available in the United States from the AEI Press, c/o Publisher Resources Inc., 1224 Heil Quaker Blvd., P.O. Box 7001, La Vergne, TN 37086-7001. Distributed outside the United States by arrangement with Eurospan, 3 Henrietta Street, London WC2E 8LU England.

Library of Congress Cataloging-in-Publication Data

Optional federal chartering and regulation of insurance companies /
    edited by Peter J. Wallison. p. cm.
  Includes bibliographical references
  ISBN 0-8447-4146-9 (pbk.: alk. paper)
    1. Insurance--United States--State supervision. 2. Insurance law--
United States. I. Wallison, Peter J.

  HG8535 .O68 2000
  368'.06'573--dc21   00-057613

The AEI Press
Publisher for the American Enterprise Institute
1150 Seventeenth Street, N.W.
Washington, D.C. 20036

Printed in the United States of America

Contents

1
Introduction
Peter J. Wallison

The June 1999 American Enterprise Institute conference on optional federal chartering and regulation of insurance companies was the first effort by a policy research organization to give extended conference exposure to an idea that had been the subject of considerable interest in the insurance industry for many years. Both the American Council of Life Insurance (ACLI) and the American Insurance Association (AIA) had revived long-dormant studies of the issue and begun to take the pulse of their members on the question of whether to proceed with a formal proposal.

The renewed interest in the idea was unusual in one respect. In the past, it had been stimulated by insurance industry problems that had come to the attention of Washington policymakers. In those cases, proposals had been floated in Washington for a federal entry into insurance regulation, and in general the insurance industry united to oppose them. Almost since it began, the industry was regulated at the state level, and its members were concerned that federal mandates and federal regulation would ultimately give them less freedom of movement and would impose greater costs than had the state system to which they had become accustomed.

This time, however, the interest in federal chartering and regulation had welled up from within the industry itself. It was the result of new competitive conditions, a reaction against excessive and unnecessary regulation, and a sense that the industry could not expand into a globalized economy if it had to seek the approval of insular state regulators for changes in products, regulation of rates, and ways of doing business. Given that rationale, it was plain that most of the pressure for a federal role in insurance regulation came from the larger companies. The smaller ones, with operations in only one or a few states, tended to think that state regulation, on balance, was good enough, and that a federal role—even though optional—could only be harmful. Nevertheless, insurance industry observers said that by 1999 there was a substantial body of industry opinion favoring optional federal chartering.

But there were some significant obstacles to proceeding. Apart from the lack of unanimity among their members, there was the delicate question of how individual companies could support federal chartering without incurring the enmity of their state regulators, who have the power to place obstacles in their paths at every turn. In addition, because of its long estrangement from the federal government, the industry had few clear advocates in Congress, or indeed Congress members who knew enough about the industry to feel comfortable supporting legislation. The same was true in the executive branch, which has no continuing connection to the industry from which it might draw internal expertise.

Further, because the issue was discussed almost exclusively within insurance industry councils—with very little discussion between associations—most members of the industry did not know where other significant players might stand on the issue. Since associations representing agents, consumers, and competitors such as banks are influential with Congress and the executive branch, it would be important to know where those organizations stood before designing legislation.

Accordingly, an AEI conference on optional federal chartering of insurance companies seemed to be a constructive contribution to the debate on that issue. Members of the insurance industry would have an opportunity to air their positions; the relevant staffs of Congress and the executive branch would get an initial exposure to the issues involved; and other interested parties—consumer groups, agents, and the banking industry—would have an opportunity to explain their positions.

This volume contains the presentations and much of the commentary delivered at the conference. It is important to note, however, that the conference was held before the enactment of the Gramm-Leach-Bliley Act in November 1999, which repealed many of the restrictions of the Glass-Steagall Act and permitted affiliations between and among banks, insurance companies, and securities firms. This did not have any effect on insurance regulation at the state level, but it accounts for references to the legislation then under consideration.

History and Background

Professor Scott Harrington of the Darla Moore School of Business, University of South Carolina, provides historical perspective in his examination of federal involvement in insurance regulation in chapter 2 of this volume. He begins by noting that the basis for state regulation was established through the Supreme Court's 1868 decision in *Paul v. Virginia*, in which the Court held that insurance was not commerce and could not be regulated by the federal government under the Commerce Clause of the Constitution. That decision both excluded the federal government from the field and confirmed the regulatory power of the states. The arrangement continued largely unchanged until 1944, when the Supreme Court overturned *Paul* with a ruling (*United States v. South-Eastern Underwriters*) that insurance is interstate commerce, and subject to the Sherman Act, when it crosses state lines.

The strong adverse reaction of the insurance industry to *South-Eastern Underwriters* produced the McCarran-Ferguson Act in 1945, with which Congress stated its intention to leave insurance regulation at the state level, and in effect to deny in advance the applicability of federal laws to the insurance industry unless those laws were expressly intended to cover insurance.

Chapter 2 traces the episodes of federal interest in insurance regulation as they arose periodically—principally as the result of insolvencies, anticompetitive practices, or other crises in the insurance industry. In each case, the federal initiative ultimately failed, but the states—frequently through the National Association of Insurance Commissioners (NAIC)—made changes in their procedures and policies that addressed some of the concerns that had given rise to the federal action. Recent examples are the adoption of risk-based capital requirements and new insolvency laws and regulations.

Mr. Harrington notes that the recent upsurge in interest in

federal chartering and regulation derives from two concerns: (1) the costs and competitive handicaps that arise in a multistate regulatory environment; and (2) the intrusiveness and pervasiveness of regulation, especially rate regulation, at the state level. Many in the industry believe that federal regulation would be less costly and more uniform than multistate regulation, and would offer the opportunity for a reduction in rate regulation. State regulators have begun to respond to those complaints.

One advantage of state regulation is that it is less likely to produce the kind of comprehensive regulatory failure that occurred in the savings and loan industry in the 1980s. In Mr. Harrington's view, if future federal regulations on the insurance industry prove to be as misguided as were those on the S&L industry, a serious problem could ensue.

Mr. Harrington concludes that the case for federal chartering is strong but not overwhelming. Whether it would be in the public interest requires an answer to three related questions:

- Could federal regulation produce material efficiencies, especially through deregulation?
- If so, is it likely that a federal system would be designed to achieve those efficiencies?
- If not, will any administrative efficiencies outweigh the risk of nationwide regulatory failure?

The Case for Federal Chartering and Regulation

This volume contains the pro and con views of spokesmen for the two segments of the insurance industry—life insurers and property and casualty insurers—because state or federal regulation would presumably affect each differently. Ironically, despite reportedly widespread support for federal chartering and regulation in both industries, it was difficult to find advocates for federal chartering and regulation. That was not necessarily because the case is weak or unpopular, but because individual insurance companies were reluctant to step forward as advocates when such a step could incur the displeasure of their current state regulators. Ultimately, only one authentic insurance company representative—speaking on behalf of a property and casualty company—would agree to appear as an advocate in favor of federal chartering and regulation. As the editor of this volume, I myself was required to state the case for federal chartering from the perspective of the life industry.

In chapter 3, Ernest T. Patrikis, senior vice president and general counsel of the American International Group, Inc., compares the system of state regulation to the European Union. There, a general agreement among the constituent countries created a regulatory regime in which an insurance company organized and regulated in one country is automatically authorized to operate in the others, with no need for separate approvals of rates or forms. If the states had been able to come together on an agreement of that kind over the years they have been in charge of insurance regulation, there would probably be no reason for this conference.

But even within the European Community, as Mr. Patrikis points out, the various countries are permitted to regulate insurance within their borders to protect "the public good." That is generally thought to refer to consumer protection, but what exactly it means, and how far countries will be permitted to go in order to protect their citizens, is still to be worked out. How it is resolved could have a profound effect on whether a single market for insurance has in fact been created within the European Community.

Mr. Patrikis concludes that there should be a federal charter option for property and casualty companies, but only for their commercial business. The potential insureds should be of such sophistication as to be able to negotiate an insurance contract on an equal footing with an insurer. There should be no form or rate regulation under that regime, and no federal guaranty fund. State laws should be preempted except to the extent that they do not frustrate the efficient operation of the insurance companies.

Such a structure would preserve the state insurance regulatory system, except in the narrow area of commercial lines. Even there, property and casualty companies would have a choice whether to remain in a state regulatory environment or to convert to a federal charter for their commercial insurance activities.

Chapter 4 of this volume, my own presentation, considers the case from the perspective of the life insurance companies. I note that the current interest in federal chartering is unusual because it is not the result of a regulatory or financial crisis in the insurance industry. But while Scott Harrington saw concern about rate regulation as a major source of insurance industry interest in federal chartering, I emphasize cross-industry competition. The difference of viewpoint probably arises because the life industry is less troubled by rate regulation than is the property and casualty industry—and at the same time it is more troubled by having to compete head-on with banks and securities firms for the public's business.

Several factors inform the life industry's support for federal chartering:

- the absence of an advocate, or even a knowledgeable voice, at the federal level;
- the success of the Comptroller of the Currency in expanding bank products through preemption of state laws;
- the effect of competition between federal and state regulators in creating a more accommodating regulatory environment for banks;
- the difficulty of expanding abroad without a regulator at the national level;
- the greater costs of regulation because of the need to comply with fifty state regulators instead of one federal regulator;
- the development of the Internet and e-commerce as a marketing vehicle not based on doing business in a particular geographic area.

Nevertheless, many thorny issues must be addressed before a viable federal chartering and regulation mechanism can be put in place. How would the state guaranty funds be integrated with a federal system? What form would a chartering and regulatory agency take, and where would it be located within the federal establishment? How would the consumer protection powers of the states be preserved? Many of those issues are addressed by other presentations in this volume.

The Case against Optional Federal Chartering

In chapter 5, Robert B. Morgan, former president and chief executive officer of Cincinnati Financial, an insurance holding company, presents the case for a state regulatory system as seen from the perspective of the property and casualty companies:

- regulators with a unique knowledge of local markets and conditions;
- flexibility and adaptability to local conditions, and an ability to reduce the impact of bad regulation, through diversity;
- promotion of innovation, because good policies spread to many other states and bad policies do not;
- less risk that a regulator who pursues bad policies will be able to affect large numbers of insurance companies;
- strong incentives to do the job effectively at the state level;
- no new federal bureaucracy;
- resources for regulation already in place.

Those elements, Mr. Morgan argues, suggest that seeking reform at the state level is preferable to setting up an entirely new system at the federal level. Moreover, a new federal system would have a number of deficiencies:

- It would create consumer confusion; consumers would not know where to lodge their complaints.
- A remote federal regulator would not be as responsive to consumer complaints as a state regulator.
- A federal regulator who is not a friend of the industry could do more harm than good.
- An alternative federal regulatory scheme would create competitive inequalities in the insurance industry and would destroy the level playing field that now exists.

Jack Wahlquist, former president and chief executive officer of Lone Star Life, offers thoughts from the life insurance companies' perspective in chapter 6. Mr. Wahlquist begins by saying that he will not attempt to defend the status quo because, in his view, the status quo is indefensible. For the current system of state regulation to survive, it must be substantially reformed. That is why the industry, as in years past, is not up in arms at the suggestion of a federal role in insurance-company regulation.

There are, in Mr. Wahlquist's view, a number of reasons for this change of view within the life industry:

- What was once thought of as the insurance industry is not that any longer; instead it is a financial-services industry, of which insurance companies are a part.

- Many of the companies are now headed by former bankers, who have experience with a different regulatory system with which they can make comparisons.
- The gradually declining importance of the agent community has reduced the pressure on life companies to oppose federal regulation.
- The federal government's role in the insurance area has been growing, starting with the Employee Retirement Income Security Act's (ERISA's) preemption of employee welfare plans, and members of Congress have not been opposing that trend. There has been no serious discussion of regulatory policy.
- State regulators have failed to understand the needs of the industry to think globally and respond quickly, and they have failed to grasp the concept of national operations.
- The NAIC has failed to overlay a national regulatory system over a state-by-state system.
- Unlike the bank regulators at the national level, the state regulators and the NAIC have failed to defend the industry's positions at the federal level.

Having said that, Wahlquist argues that the best defense against a system of dual regulation is a dramatic and substantial reform of the current system of state regulation. If the necessary steps are taken at the state level, he believes the industry will once again be united in defending the state system against a federal incursion.

Chapter 7 presents remarks by Jack Chesson, senior legislative counsel of the National Association of Insurance Commissioners. Mr. Chesson notes that creating a federal role in insurance chartering and regulation is much easier discussed than done. For one thing, state governors will be strongly opposed, since insurance regulation and taxation provide a major source of state revenues. In addition, there is a significant question about where the insurance regulator would be located in the federal government—a question that has major jurisdictional implications for congressional committees.

But quite apart from those matters, Mr. Chesson argues, the NAIC is moving now to address the issues that gave rise to the federal chartering idea in the first place. The NAIC understands that it is necessary to create both uniformity and efficiency of regulation at the state level and to work cooperatively with the federal government.

Those new initiatives will reinforce the advantages that state regulation already confers, especially in the area of consumer protection. The fact that the state regulatory system exists, and is now reforming itself to do its job more effectively, will mean that Congress is not going to leap into the unknown with a program of federal regulation.

Cost Comparisons

One of the key elements of the case for federal chartering is the view among proponents that a fifty-state regulatory system is very costly to companies that operate nationally. The cost of maintaining a compliance staff for fifty states, and applying for approvals from fifty regulators, is frequently cited as one of the reasons to create a single federal chartering and regulatory agency.

In chapter 8, Professors Martin F. Grace and Robert W. Klein of the Center for Risk Management and Insurance Research, Georgia State University, present the results of their co-written study. The chapter begins with a discussion of why insurance is regulated, an inquiry that establishes a baseline of regulatory activity against which to compare the costs of state and hypothetical federal regulation. One of the important reasons for regulation, according to Professors Grace and Klein, is to protect consumers, who find it costly to acquire the information necessary to make informed decisions. A second reason is to protect those whose losses might not be compensated because of the inability or unwillingness of insured parties to make informed decisions concerning the meaning of insurance contracts or the solvency of an insurance carrier.

Professors Grace and Klein assume that an optional federal chartering system would permit federally chartered insurance companies to sell insurance in any state, and a federal charter would preempt all state regulation regarding financial supervision or regulation of an insurance company, as well as its market practices. State insurers would be regulated much as they are now, with a license required in every state in which they do business and the solvency regulator being the state of domicile.

Because the states generally rely on a company's domiciliary state for solvency regulation, moving to a federal system of regulation would not result in significant cost savings to insurers. Some savings would occur at the state level because of the reduced need to duplicate the solvency regulation infrastructure in each state, but those savings would be reduced if a number of insurers remained as state-chartered institutions.

Yet because each state regulates the operations of insurers within its borders, significant savings could occur among the states if rates and forms were no longer regulated—or regulated as heavily—at the state level. That would result in a substantial reduction in personnel.

As to the compliance costs of insurers in a state regulation system, those generally consist of the following: submitting applications for licensing, submitting financial and statistical reports, paying for audits and examinations, preparing and submitting rates and forms filings, ensuring internal compliance with state regulations, responding to regulatory inquiries, and paying taxes, fees, and assessments. Of those, the filing of separate licensing applications in each of fifty states is probably the most costly activity, and the costs of complying with individual state market regulations and procedures are also high.

The data in chapter 8 show that the larger the number of states in which an insurer is licensed, the higher the compliance expenses of the insurer relative to premiums—a relationship called an expense ratio. The increased expenses differ between property and casualty companies on the one hand and life companies on the other. The expense ratios of life companies will generally rise more quickly than those of property and casualty companies as the number of state licenses increase. The evidence presented in chapter 8 suggests that regulatory costs are associated with nonessential regulation in the life insurance industry, because of restrictive regulatory environments.

The problem of nonessential regulation suggests that there could be significant compliance-cost reductions in a federal chartering and regulatory system, if the federal authority were to reduce nonessential regulation and nonuniform state conduct regulation not beneficial to the public.

Professors Grace and Klein note, however, that a rough estimate of total compliance cost for the insurance industry as a whole would be $4.5 billion, representing less than one percent of industry premiums. That suggests that, no matter how efficient federal chartering and regulation, the savings to the industry would not be large relative to total premiums.

Moreover, any cost savings in that area are likely to be considerably smaller than the savings from eliminating nonessential market regulations and standardizing the regulations that are retained. Accordingly, at least in terms of cost, insurance regulatory policies are probably more important than determining whether chartering and regulation occur at the federal or the state level.

Regulatory Issues—The Devil Is in the Details

The creation of a federal chartering and regulatory regime for insurance companies is easy to conceive in principle but may be difficult to implement in practice. Numerous issues involving politically complex decisions would have to be resolved. Two chapters in this volume reflect the scope of the difficulties to be addressed by lawmakers.

In chapter 9, Bert Ely of Ely & Co. addresses the issues to be considered when existing state guaranty funds are integrated with a federally operated guaranty fund. First, Mr. Ely observes that if there is federal chartering and regulation there will also have to be some form of federal guarantee of the solvency of federally chartered insurance companies. For a variety of reasons, the federal government cannot assume responsibility for insurance company solvency without having some mechanism in place for paying the costs of insolvencies when they occur.

Mr. Ely then reviews the history and structures of the state guaranty funds, pointing out that their functions and total coverages differ from state to state. Areas of difference include how the funds are administered; whether there is a fund balance or an obligation on the part of participating insurers to pay into a fund when a loss occurs; which product lines are protected and which are not; and whether payments on the guarantee can be passed on to taxpayers through offsets. Surprisingly for the insurance industry, there is almost no risk sensitivity in the guaranty fund assessments required of insurers.

The following are some of the key policy questions with respect to guaranty funds that Congress, in Mr. Ely's view, would have to address in connection with the establishment of a system for the federal chartering of insurance companies:

- whether to rely on the state guaranty funds or to establish a federal fund or guaranty system; the likelihood is that Congress would adopt a federal system;
- whether state-chartered companies would be allowed to join the federal guaranty fund program;
- whether to give the Federal Deposit Insurance Corporation (FDIC) control over the federal guaranty fund or to establish a new administrative agency for that purpose;
- whether to maintain a minimum fund balance or to assess participating insurers when a loss occurs;
- whether insurance companies, like insured banks, should have access to the Fed's discount window in the event of liquidity difficulties;
- what product lines to protect, and the maximum amount of guaranty fund coverages;
- how fund assessments should be calculated—whether on the basis of total premiums of the guaranteed company or on a risk-based formula.

Each of those decisions carries difficult sub-issues. For example, if Congress elects to allow all state-chartered companies to join the federal guarantee fund system, it may drive the state systems out of business. But if it allows only well-capitalized and well-managed companies, the state funds will be left with the greatest risks. Also, if the federal guaranty fund is responsible for losses by state-chartered companies, would the federal government not have to assume solvency regulation for state-chartered insurers or, at a minimum, subject them to dual supervision?

Finally, Mr. Ely notes that when Congress is considering the establishment of a federal guaranty fund, it might consider a completely privatized system, in which insurance companies guarantee one another's liabilities in exchange for a risk-based premium. Such a system would take solvency regulation for participating insurance companies out of the hands of both the federal government and the states.

In chapter 10, Robert C. Eager and Cantwell F. Muckenfuss, both of Gibson, Dunn & Crutcher, present a variety of other issues. Messrs. Eager and Muckenfuss identify what they see as the major political and policy issues associated with the establishment of a federal chartering and regulatory system for insurance companies. Their list of issues includes the following:

- the scope of the federal charter—that is, whether it will encompass comprehensive chartering for all areas of insurance activity or limited to specified ones; whether it will cover all activities of federally chartered insurers or will leave portions of their activities still covered by state regulators;
- whether preemption of state laws will require specific action by the federal regulator—where state laws conflict with federal laws or policies—or will be automatic and comprehensive, so that federal insurance companies will not be subject to any restrictions unless imposed at the federal level;
- the structure and position of the insurance regulator within the federal establishment—whether to place the agency as a bureau within a federal department or to structure it as an independent agency, and whether to have it headed by a single administrator or a multimember commission;
- how to structure conversion from a state to a federal charter, and whether to provide for a federal mutual charter;
- whether to provide for federal regulation of insurance holding companies, even if those entities do not also control banks;
- whether to subject federally chartered insurance companies to federal policies and laws that apply to banks—for example, the Community Reinvestment Act;
- finally, and perhaps most important, whether to use the process of creating a new insurance regulatory system as an opportunity to approach the whole question of insurance regulation from a new and market-oriented perspective.

The Views of Other Stakeholders

Insurance companies are not the only institutions and groups that have an interest in the shape of insurance regulation in the future. Insurance agents certainly have an interest in how the industry is regulated, as do consumers. Interestingly, in a competitive world where banks and insurance companies are both members of a larger financial-services industry, banks are also concerned about how insurance companies are regulated. Accordingly, this volume includes the views of representatives of agents' groups, consumers, and an affiliate of the American Bankers Association that has been developing draft legislation that would create a federal chartering option for insurance companies.

Broker Organizations. In chapter 11, Joel Wood, of the Council of Insurance Agents and Brokers, speaks from the vantage point of larger brokers and broker organizations. Mr. Wood's organization, which generally represents brokers who operate interstate, supported a provision of H.R. 10 and S. 900—the financial industry reform legislation enacted in November 1999—that created a national self-regulatory organization for insurance brokers. That organization, known as the National Association of Registered Agents and Brokers (NARAB), would come into effect only if the states do create uniform standards for agents and brokers within a specified time period.

In his presentation, Mr. Wood outlines the reasons why his organization thought some kind of federal action was necessary, at least as a spur to state action. He notes that state regulation does not generally affect the agents who sell personal lines, either independently or for large insurers, since those agents seldom sell in more than one or two states. For agents and brokers in the commercial lines, however—especially those who customarily sell on a nationwide basis—the current system requires licenses to be obtained on a line-by-line, class-by-class, producer-by-producer, state-by-state basis. That system usually requires a single agent or broker to hold scores of licenses. An agent or broker marketing a national insurance program may routinely have to obtain more than 100 licenses.

In addition, some states have residency requirements for brokers, or they require that brokers incorporate their agencies in the state in which they are selling. Those requirements not only are a burden on agents and brokers but can be highly anti-

competitive and create unnecessary costs that are eventually
passed on to consumers.

More broadly, Mr. Wood notes, the policies underlying the
McCarran-Ferguson Act should be reviewed. It was adopted in
1945, when the business of insurance was predominantly local in
character. Much has changed since then; the insurance market
has become national and even global. Indeed, even the Comptroller of the Currency has recognized that fact by permitting insurance subsidiaries of banks in towns of fewer than 5,000 to sell
their products anywhere in the world. Moreover, insurance products are now just one aspect of a broader, globalized financial-
services business—which itself requires a broader and more
global view of insurance regulation, especially on the commercial
side. For those reasons, Woods concludes, the Council of Insurance Agents and Brokers will support an optional federal charter
for insurance companies.

Independent Agents. In chapter 12, the National Association
of Life Underwriters (NALU), an organization of smaller and independent agents, takes a different view. According to Michael
Kerley, senior vice president of government affairs for NALU,
the purpose of regulation in the insurance field is to ensure the
good reputations of insurance agents and companies. In that, he
believes, the states have succeeded.

It is understandable that the larger organizations would see
a need for federal-level chartering. The surprising revelation to
Mr. Kerley is that the academics do not believe the advantages
of federal chartering to be overwhelming; in general, their support for the idea has been tepid. He notes in his remarks that the
members of his organization have found that dealing with a local
regulator is better for them and for their clients. To the extent
that local regulation creates problems for larger organizations,
he believes the NAIC is beginning to respond—in part because of
conferences like that held at AEI in 1999, upon which this volume is based. Accordingly, Mr. Kerley is optimistic that the
NAIC will come to grips with the problems associated with multistate regulation, without the need for a federal chartering option.

A Consumer Perspective. In chapter 13, J. Robert Hunter, director of insurance for the Consumer Federation of America, sug-

gests that Congress conduct a one-year study of federal chartering, addressing such issues as the following:

- the regulatory functions necessary to obtain effective pro-consumer insurance regulation;
- how well the current system has served consumers;
- whether there are changes underway in the insurance market that make a new approach preferable;
- the proper roles of the federal government and the states in insurance regulation.

Mr. Hunter outlines the functions he believes insurance regulation should entail, and he reviews the performance of the states in each area. He concludes that the states have not been effective regulators from the standpoint of consumers. On the question of whether trends are underway that imply changes in regulatory structure, he notes that several factors will impede effective management by the states. Those include international trade agreements, the sale of insurance over the Internet, international mergers, the breach of the walls separating the various financial-services providers, and competition among the states to attract insurance providers. As to the appropriate federal role, Mr. Hunter believes that is a subject for Congress to study.

He concludes that, in light of the major trends he describes, and the signs of strain at the state level, the federal government has an obligation to review the policies underlying the McCarran-Ferguson Act.

The Banking Industry. In chapter 14, Larry LaRocco, managing director of the ABA Insurance Association, presents a view from the banking industry. The ABA Insurance Association is an affiliate of the American Bankers Association; its bank members are all actively engaged in the sale of insurance. The organization monitors insurance developments at the state level and develops and proposes necessary legislation.

Mr. LaRocco notes that one of the long-term objectives of the ABAIA is the federal regulation of insurance. The organization's members believe that a single federal regulator will simplify compliance requirements and stimulate the development of uniform products. To further that objective, the ABAIA has been preparing draft legislation that would create an optional federal chartering and regulatory agency for insurance. The legislation is not yet complete, and his comments below should be understood in that context, but its principal terms are the following:

- A federal insurance commissioner would be established as a single-headed agency within the Department of the Treasury.
- The commissioner would be authorized to charter, examine, supervise, and regulate federal insurance companies— authority patterned after the powers of the Office of Thrift Supervision under the Homeowners Loan Act.
- Charters would be granted only to companies that seek them; becoming a federal insurance company would be optional.
- The commissioner would be empowered to establish supervisory and consumer standards. Supervisory standards would include requirements and standards for capital, liquidity, investment and lending, and accounting and valuation. Consumer standards would include market conduct regulations covering such things as false advertising, discrimination, claims practice, and tie-in sales.
- A Federal Insurance Guaranty Corporation would maintain two funds—one for life and health liabilities and one for property and casualty liabilities. The funds would be financed by regular assessments on insurance companies.
- The commissioner would be prohibited from regulating rates, and federal insurance companies or agencies would be subject to the antitrust laws.
- The commissioner's office would be funded by assessments and fees paid by the insurance industry.

In summary, LaRocco and the ABAIA support an optional system of federal chartering and regulation of insurance.

PART ONE
Historical Overview

2
The History of Federal Involvement in Insurance Regulation

Scott E. Harrington

The Commerce Clause of the U.S. Constitution authorizes the federal government to regulate interstate commerce. The Tenth Amendment reserves powers to the states and to the people that are neither delegated to the federal government by the Constitution nor prohibited to the states. Supreme Court interpretations of these provisions during much of the twentieth century have contributed to an enormous expansion of federal legislation and regulation. State insurance regulation is an interesting exception to the increasingly broad sweep of federal legislation and regulation. In contrast to banking, where federal chartering was permitted in 1864 as part of legislation regulating the national currency, regulation of insurance lies primarily with the states. Insurers are chartered at the state level and are subject to rules and regulation in each state where they conduct business.

The history of insurance regulation is characterized by a series of perceived market or regulatory failures, followed by threats of federal regulation and subsequent changes by the states that have helped forestall federal action. Pressure is once again beginning to mount for some form of federal chartering or regulation, in principle to achieve efficiencies in the regulation of multistate insurers (and agents). Whether the preeminence of state regulation in insurance will survive long beyond the end of the twentieth century is uncertain.

At one level of analysis, the debate over insurance regulation involves the fundamental considerations addressed by the framers of the Constitution and eloquently set forth by Hamilton and Madison in the *Federalist Papers*. Persons who adhere to the view that power should be delegated to the smallest unit of government that can develop and administer policy effectively have generally been sympathetic to state insurance regulation. The philosophical basis for state regulation appears to be eroding, however, as modern developments suggest potentially greater efficiencies from increased centralization of regulatory authority. At a more pragmatic level, insurance industry support for state regulation has partially eroded, in large part because of a desire for limited deregulation. Insurer support for some form of federal chartering and regulation varies in more or less predictable ways by type and size of company.

This chapter provides a historical overview of federal involvement, both legislative and judicial, in insurance regulation and in proposals for federal chartering and regulation. I first provide a thumbnail sketch of the history of insurance regulation. I then describe several key episodes since the 1960s that led to proposals for modifying federal law concerning insurance regulation, and to subsequent reactions by state regulators. Following is a consideration of sources of support for state versus federal regulation and factors that have altered the mix of support over time. I conclude with brief comments on some of the key issues and risks presented by increased centralization of insurance regulation.[1]

How We Arrived

A newcomer to the history of insurance regulation might regard the basic facts as remarkably strange. From the U.S. Supreme Court's early decision that insurance is not commerce, through its 1995 decision that fixed annuities are not insurance, the key developments of insurance regulation at first impression might seem to defy logical explanations. However, the real anomaly may instead be that the states have thus far largely prevailed in the nearly 150-year struggle over insurance regulation.

State regulation of insurance companies and agents began to develop in the early part of the nineteenth century. The primary source of regulation was restrictions and limitations concerning insurer operations contained in state charters issued to insurers that allowed them to conduct business. Domestic insurers were required to file annual reports as early as 1818, beginning in Massachusetts. The first state insurance department (commission) was established in New Hampshire in 1851; other states soon followed suit.

Bills that would have created a federal agency to regulate insurance were introduced in the U.S. Congress in the 1860s, but they were not enacted. As noted earlier, the Commerce Clause of the U.S. Constitution gives the federal government explicit authority to regulate interstate commerce, and the Tenth Amendment to the Constitution states that powers not delegated to the federal government are reserved to the states. The interpretation of those provisions in the twentieth century that led to the broad expansion of federal powers occurred much later than the formative years of insurance regulation, when the insurance business was considered to be "local" (that is, conducted within a state) rather than interstate commerce.

***Paul v. Virginia:* Insurance Is Not Commerce.** The question of whether states had the power to regulate insurance was addressed in 1868 by the U.S. Supreme Court in the celebrated case of *Paul v. Virginia* (75 U.S. 168). Mr. Paul was an agent for a group of New York fire insurers. Virginia law required out-of-state insurers and their agents to be licensed by the state. Mr. Paul refused to pay the security deposit that was required to obtain a license; he continued to sell policies, and then he was fined. Mr. Paul and the New York insurers challenged the conviction, arguing in part that the sale of insurance across borders was interstate commerce and thus that the Virginia law was unconstitutional, because it interfered with interstate commerce. The Court held instead that insurance was not commerce and therefore was not subject to laws affecting interstate commerce. Virginia's law was not unconstitutional. States, rather than the federal government, had the power to regulate insurance. That decision was upheld for approximately seventy-five years in a number of other cases that argued that insurance constituted interstate commerce.

Unregulated Price Fixing and the South-Eastern Underwriters Association Decision. During the 1870s, numerous insurance companies became insolvent in part because of major fires in Boston and Chicago. Those events spurred the development of insurance-rating bureaus, precursor organizations to modern rate-advisory organizations (such as the Insurance Services Office). The rating bureaus set property insurance rates that would be charged by most companies, in principle to ensure adequate prices and therefore reduce insolvency risk. Many states either permitted or encouraged the development of rating bureaus; some states began to regulate their activities. Regulators in a few states set rates for use by all companies.

In response to a request from the Missouri attorney general in 1942, the Antitrust Division of the U.S. Department of Justice began an investigation into the activities of a large rating bureau known as the South-Eastern Underwriters Association. That association was subsequently indicted by the U.S. attorney general for alleged violations of the Sherman Antitrust Act. The charges included restraining and monopolizing commerce, fixing prices and agents' commissions, attempting to force buyers to buy from member insurers, denying nonmember insurers access to reinsurance from member insurers, and refusing to transact with agents who represented nonmember insurers.

The South-Eastern Underwriters Association (SEUA) argued that many of those practices were beneficial, given the nature of insurance. But its defense against that legal action was that the Sherman act did not apply to insurance because insurance was not commerce according to *Paul v. Virginia*. A federal district court upheld that view and dismissed the case. The U.S. attorney general appealed to the Supreme Court.

The Court did not decide on the merit of the charges, but in *United States v. South-Eastern Underwriters Association* (322 U.S. 533, 1944), it overturned *Paul v. Virginia* by a four-to-three vote with two justices not voting. The majority basically ruled that insurance is commerce, that it is interstate commerce when it takes place across state lines, that Congress could therefore regulate insurance, and that the Sherman Antitrust Act applied to insurance. The decision did not prohibit state regulation, but it held that state laws contrary to federal law were invalid. Chief

Justice Harlan Stone's dissent (joined by that of Justice Felix Frankfurter) argued that the Congress never intended the antitrust laws to apply to insurance. Justice Robert Jackson agreed that insurance was commerce but rejected the majority's use of the Sherman act to "strike down the constitutional basis of state regulation."

The McCarran-Ferguson Act. The SEUA decision produced considerable uncertainty about the allowable scope of state regulation and taxation of insurers. It also created considerable uncertainty about the legality of industry operating procedures, especially the use of rating bureaus. Representatives of both the insurance industry and state regulation sought federal legislation to clarify regulatory and taxation issues related to insurance. The Congress swiftly enacted the McCarran-Ferguson Act in 1945 (15 U.S.C., 1945). The act states that the continued regulation and taxation of insurance by the states is in the public interest. In what is often called "reverse preemption," the act states that no act of Congress "shall be construed to invalidate, impair, or supersede" any state law enacted for the purpose of regulating or taxing insurance. However, the law goes on to state that the Sherman, Clayton, and Federal Trade Commission Acts "shall be applicable to the business of insurance to the extent that such business is not regulated by state law," and that the Sherman act is applicable to "any agreement to boycott, coerce, or intimidate, or act of boycott, coercion, or intimidation."[2]

The implications of that legislation were clear. First, states would continue to have primary authority for insurance regulation, although the federal government could enact legislation regulating insurance if state regulation were found to be deficient. Second, many of the activities of rating bureaus would not be subject to federal antitrust law, provided they were regulated by the states and did not involve boycott, coercion, or intimidation.

Most states revised their regulatory systems to provide greater oversight of rating-bureau activities following the enactment of the McCarran-Ferguson Act. The most common approach was to make property-liability insurance rates developed by rating bureaus subject to regulatory prior approval. The laws generally either required or strongly encouraged all insurers to use bureau rates. Beginning in the late 1950s, however, most states began to make it easier for insurers to charge rates that differed from bureau rates, and the large direct writers generally obtained approval to charge lower rates. Beginning in the mid-1960s, a significant number of states ultimately eliminated prior-approval regulation, replacing their prior-approval laws with competitive rating laws. Modern insurance advisory organizations now commonly file prospective loss costs with state regulators (as opposed to final rates) that can be used by insurers in their own rate filings. State oversight of those activities has generally been sufficient to keep them from being subject to federal antitrust law.[3]

A second but slower response to the McCarran-Ferguson Act was the states' enactment of legislation dealing with unfair trade practices by insurers to deter application of the FTC act to insurance. In *Federal Trade Commission v. National Casualty Co.* (357 U.S. 560, 1957), the Supreme Court rejected FTC regulation of insurer advertising. In a much later case, *FTC v. Ticor Title Insurance Co.* (112 S.Ct. 2169, 1992), the Court permitted an FTC challenge to the fixing of rates for title services. Following FTC studies of the insurance industry in the late 1970s, in 1980 Congress exempted the business of insurance from the FTC's investigative and reporting powers (except those related to antitrust violations). FTC studies and reports on insurance were permitted only when requested by a majority of specified congressional committees.

Numerous additional Court decisions have interpreted the scope of the McCarran-Ferguson Act's antitrust protection for the "business of insurance" and the meaning of "boycott."[4] The ultimate trend was toward narrowing the antitrust exemption by narrowing the scope of activities regarded as the business of insurance (for example, *Group Life & Health Insurance Co. v. Royal Drug Co.,* 440 U.S. 205, 1979) and by broadening the meaning of boycott (for example, *St. Paul Fire & Marine v. Barry,* 438 U.S. 531, 1978, and *Hartford Fire v. California,* 113 S.Ct. 2891, 1993). Moreover, the Court narrowed the meaning of insurance in two key cases involving the extension of federal regulation to insurance-related activities. In *SEC v. VALIC of America* (359 U.S. 65, 1959), the Court held that variable annuities were securities and not insurance and therefore were subject to federal securities laws, including SEC regulation. In *NationsBank v. VALIC* (115 S.Ct. 810, 1995), the Court held that the fixed annuities were part of the business of banking and not insurance, thereby upholding a decision by the Comptroller of the Currency permitting national banks to sell annuities. The Court's ruling facilitated substantial expansion in bank sales of annuities.

Because of Court decisions and specific federal legislation, federal law and regulation currently affect insurance in many areas besides this brief sampling. Examples include application of the Fair Housing Act to alleged insurance redlining, Racketeer Influenced Corrupt Organizations (RICO) suits against insurers, federal authorization of risk-retention and risk-purchasing groups, and the complex issue of preemption under ERISA.

Federal Threats and State Reactions

Congress has exerted substantial pressure on state regulators to change regulatory practices by periodically threatening to adopt some form of federal regulation. To be sure, it is difficult to disentangle the extent to which changes in state regulation are undertaken to deter federal regulation. But even a casual reading of the evidence suggests that state regulators are influenced by the threat of federal intervention. The following section examines several episodes that illustrate the interplay between proposed federal regulation and state responses.

Insolvencies and the Development of State Guaranty Funds. Property-liability insurance-company insolvencies received considerable attention in the late 1960s. Many of the insurers that failed had specialized in providing auto-liability insurance in the nonstandard market (that is, to high-risk or relatively low-income buyers). Concern with those insolvencies produced criticism of state regulation and a congressional proposal for a federal guaranty system patterned after deposit insurance.

State regulators responded in several ways. Most important, the National Association of Insurance Commissioners (NAIC) adopted model legislation for state guaranty funds in 1969 and 1970. The state guaranty fund system for property-liability insurance expanded rapidly in the 1970s; guaranty fund growth was slower for life-health insurers. In both cases, however, most states eventually passed legislation that is identical or substantially similar to the model legislation. The NAIC also developed an early warning system for the detection of financially weak insurers by state regulators (the Insurance Regulatory Information System), which was implemented in 1974.

The 1960s insolvencies and a subsequent increase in insolvencies in the property-liability insurance industry during the mid-1970s also influenced Senator Edward Brooke of Massachusetts to propose a system of dual federal and state regulation. That bill (S. 3884, Federal Insurance Act, introduced October 1976) would have allowed optional federal chartering and regulation of insurers with full preemption of state regulation. It also would have created a federal guaranty fund analogous to deposit insurance. As I discuss below, a variation on this approach resurfaced in the early 1990s.

Insurance Affordability and the Liability Insurance Crisis. During the mid-1980s and early 1990s, significant support for modifying or eliminating the limited exemption of the business of insurance from federal antitrust law arose in conjunction with rapid increases in property-liability insurance rates. Real auto insurance rates grew rapidly (see figure 2–1) in conjunction with rapid growth in claim costs. Probably more important, the liability insurance crisis of the mid-1980s produced sharp increases in commercial liability insurance rates and premiums following a period of declining premiums and worsening insurer operating margins during the early 1980s (see figure 2–2). The chronic real increases in auto insurance rates and sharp increases in commercial liability-insurance rates focused renewed attention on the efficacy of the McCarran-Ferguson Act's exemption.

Some observers argued that the insurance industry's limited exemption from antitrust law facilitated collusion among insurers to increase prices, especially in the context of the liability insurance crisis. There are two main counterarguments. First, unless prevented by price regulation, property-liability insurance markets are characterized by substantial heterogeneity in prices and underwriting standards. That heterogeneity is, prima facie, inconsistent with price fixing. Second, advisory organizations in principle can help promote healthy competition and

FIGURE 2–1

CONSUMER PRICE INDEXES FOR AUTOMOBILE INSURANCE
AND FOR ALL ITEMS, 1981–1997

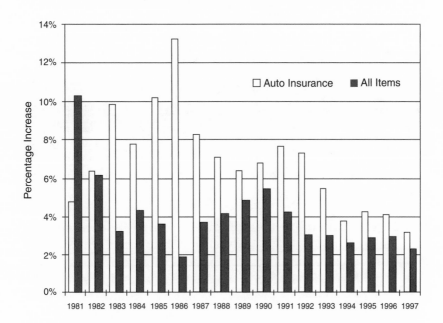

thereby benefit consumers by providing valuable, low-cost information concerning projected loss costs. The availability at low
cost of loss forecasts based on aggregate industry data, when
combined with an insurer's own data analysis, helps many insurers predict losses more accurately, thus reducing insurer risk
and the need for capital. It also reduces the cost of ratemaking
and entry into a particular market or line of business.

The development of advisory rates and policy forms by the
Insurance Services Office (ISO) nonetheless became the subject
of considerable controversy during and following the 1980s increases in liability-insurance premiums. As pressure mounted
for modification in the industry's limited antitrust exemption,
the attorneys general of nearly twenty states filed a federal antitrust suit against the ISO, the Reinsurance Association of
America, and a number of other domestic and non-U.S. insurers
and reinsurers. The suit alleged illegal activity associated with
the introduction of a new standard general liability insurance

FIGURE 2–2
GENERAL LIABILITY INSURANCE NET PREMIUMS AND
OPERATING MARGINS, 1978–1997

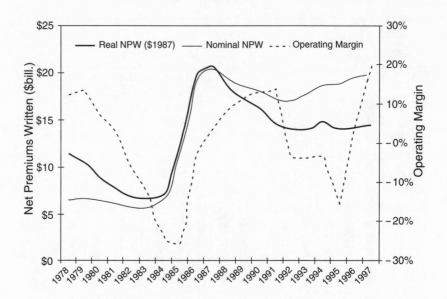

contract in the mid-1980s. It was settled after the Supreme
Court refused to dismiss the case, ruling inter alia in 1993 that
some of the alleged activities would constitute a boycott if proved
to have occurred.

State regulators responded to the events of the mid-to-late
1980s, including criticisms of rate-advisory organization activities, in two main ways. First, in 1989 an NAIC committee proposed prohibiting the promulgation by rate-service organizations
of advisory rates that included expense and profit loadings. The
ISO in effect complied voluntarily and instead disseminated only
developed and trended loss costs. Second, a number of states
switched to loss-cost systems or prohibited the use of advisory
rates or loss costs in rate filings by insurers with market shares
above specified thresholds.

Representative Jack Brooks of Texas and Senator Howard
Metzenbaum of Ohio eventually proposed bills that would have
substantially eliminated the industry's antitrust exemption. For
example, the Brooks bill (H.R. 9, the Insurance Competitive Pric-

ing Act of 1994, reported to the House in October 1994) would have amended the McCarran-Ferguson Act to eliminate the anti-trust exemption except for specified safe harbors, including conduct involving historical loss data and loss development, standard policy forms, and risk pools that historically provided underwriting capacity. Pressure for modifying the antitrust exemption subsequently declined as premium growth abated and the key advocates left Congress.

Insolvency Problems and Guaranty Funds Revisited. The early 1990s saw another challenge to state regulation, again in response to increases in the frequency and severity of insurance company insolvencies. Figure 2–3 shows, by sector, the number of property-liability insurers and life-health insurers declared insolvent each year during the period 1981–1996. It also shows assessments by state insurance guaranty funds against surviving insurers (in constant 1996 dollars) to pay some of the claims against insolvent insurers.[5] Beginning in the mid-1980s, the number of insurer insolvencies increased significantly compared with historical norms. The increase in the number of insolvencies and an increase in the average size of insolvent insurers substantially increased guaranty fund assessments.

The largest insolvent property-liability insurer to date (Mission Insurance Group in 1987) ranked among the top fifty insurers in total premiums and among the top ten in workers' compensation insurance premiums prior to its insolvency. The Mission insolvency required guaranty fund assessments of nearly $500 million. Several other insolvent property-liability insurers have required assessments of $250 million or more. Several relatively large life insurers failed in 1991, including two insurer groups that ranked in the top twenty-five in terms of assets (Executive Life and Mutual Benefit Life). Guaranty fund assessments for Executive Life totaled $2.1 billion, more than five times greater than for any other life-health insurer insolvency.[6]

The increase in the frequency and severity of insurer insolvencies generated concern about the quality of state solvency regulation. The 1990 report, *Failed Promises*, based on hearings held by Representative John Dingell of Michigan, contained a scathing indictment of alleged defects in state solvency regulation. The

FIGURE 2–3
INSURER INSOLVENCIES AND GUARANTY FUND ASSESSMENTS, 1981–1996
(in constant $1996)

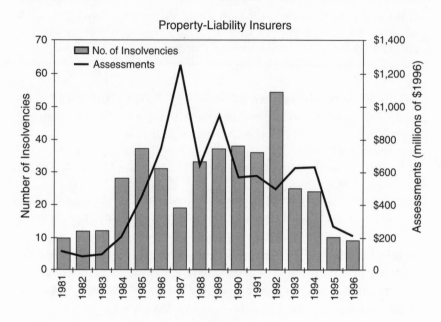

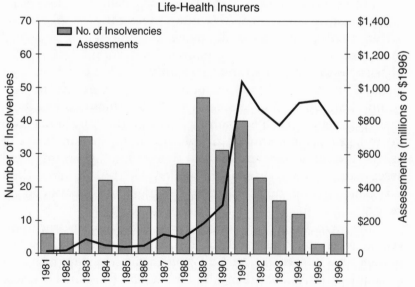

General Accounting Office also issued several reports that were highly critical of state solvency regulation. In 1993 Representative Dingell introduced a bill (H.R. 1290, the Federal Insurance Solvency Act of 1993) that would have created a dual system of state and federal solvency regulation. Specifically, the bill would:

- create a Federal Insurance Solvency Commission (FISC) to establish preemptive federal standards for state solvency regulation;
- allow insurers to become federally "certified" and thus be subject to solvency regulation by the FISC rather than the states;
- make reinsurers subject to FISC regulation;
- create a prefunded federal guaranty system for federally certified insurers;
- exempt highly capitalized, commercial-line insurers with federal certification from state regulation of rates, forms, and unfair trade and settlement practices;
- establish a uniform system for the multistate licensing of agents and brokers.

The Dingell bill was criticized on a variety of accounts, including the proposed federal guaranty system and bifurcation of solvency and rate regulation. Moreover, the Dingell and GAO reports notwithstanding, many factors apart from possible regulatory failure contributed to the increase in insurer insolvencies during the late 1980s and early 1990s. Many property-liability insurers that failed during the 1980s wrote large amounts of business liability insurance, including product liability, environmental liability, and professional liability insurance. Those insolvencies were associated with much higher claim costs than the insurers originally reported on their financial statements. A large component of the increase in claim costs was probably unexpected in many cases; that is, significantly higher than could reasonably have been expected when the insurers wrote the business and initially reported estimates of claim costs.

Some property-liability insurer insolvencies during the mid-to-late 1980s were probably influenced by intense competition that characterized the soft market for business liability insurance during the early 1980s. A large increase in market interest rates in the late 1970s and early 1980s may also have contrib-

uted to some insolvencies. Higher interest rates substantially reduced the market value of bonds held by many insurers. Some
companies might have been weakened to the point that they engaged in go-for-broke behavior that may have been difficult to
detect by regulators until it was too late to prevent large losses.

The increase in the frequency of life-health insurer insolvencies that began in the mid-1980s was attributable in part to
small health insurers that experienced large claim costs in relation to premiums and the claim liabilities that they originally
reported. The insolvency of several large life insurance companies in 1991 was more consequential and accounted for much of
the increase in guaranty fund assessments. The large life insurer
insolvencies primarily reflected reductions in the value of assets
held, including Executive Life, which had invested heavily in
high-yield bonds. The more widespread problem was the reduction in real estate values, which, for example, precipitated the
insolvency of Mutual Benefit Life.

The insolvencies of Executive Life, Mutual Benefit Life, and
a few other insurers were preceded by substantial cash withdrawals by life insurance and annuity policyholders who had ac-
cumulated savings with these insurers and who had become
concerned with the safety of their funds. There was significant
concern during the spring and summer of 1991 that large numbers of life insurance and annuity policyholders might panic and
attempt to withdraw funds from other insurers that were not
experiencing significant financial problems. No other large insurer failed in 1991, however, and asset values subsequently re-
bounded in many cases, which markedly strengthened the
capital of the industry.[7] Whether some regulators took action
against some insurers prematurely or made statements that un-
duly frightened policyholders and contributed to the insolvency
of others is subject to debate.

Following the events of 1991, many life insurers raised new
capital and improved the quality of their assets. Evidence suggests that policyholder withdrawals of funds during 1990 and
1991 occurred primarily for weak companies, as opposed to reflecting irrational panic and contagion that adversely affected
strong insurers. Many policyholders appear to have become more
concerned with insurer safety during that time. The resulting

flight to quality provided additional incentives for insurers to increase their capital and reduce risk.

State regulators responded to the insolvency experience, federal criticism, and potential federal legislation by taking numerous actions to strengthen solvency regulation. One key change was the development by the NAIC of risk-based capital requirements, which followed that step in banking regulation. A second important development was the NAIC's adoption of a solvency-regulation accreditation program, which led many states to change their solvency laws and regulation to comply with the standards promulgated by the NAIC. Substantial debate occurred about the efficacy of those measures and, more generally, about the need for and appropriate means of achieving greater centralization in solvency regulation—whether through the NAIC, with little or no enforcement power, or through federal regulation or the creation of a legally binding interstate compact. Support for federal intervention waned in conjunction with changes that were made in state regulation and, perhaps serendipitously for state regulators, as insolvency experience improved.

Politics, Price Regulation, and Bureaucracy. More recent debate on the efficacy of state regulation has focused heavily on the direct and indirect costs of state regulation of prices, policy forms, and producer licensing. There are two key issues. First, costs and delays incurred by multistate insurers that must deal with multiple and often conflicting state rules and procedures have assumed greater importance in an environment of financial modernization, growing electronic commerce, and global competition. While especially relevant to life-annuity and multiline insurers who seek to provide a diversified array of financial services, the issue is also important for commercial-line property-liability insurers who face increasing competition from alternative risk-transfer mechanisms. Federal regulation is viewed by some observers as offering the potential for reductions in the direct and indirect costs of regulation through less intrusive and more uniform regulation. Potential efficiencies from greater centralization and uniformity have always favored some form of national regulation.

The second key issue is the tendency of state price regulation both to constrain rate increases below cost increases during periods of rapid growth in claim costs and to promote cross-subsidies among groups of insurance buyers. Those policies have developed largely because of political demands for regulators somehow to make insurance more affordable. Strong political pressure to limit rate increases exposes insurers to material risk of loss during inflationary cost surges, even though such policies are unsustainable in the long run without inducing substantial exit by insurers. Marginally sustainable cross-subsidy schemes, which force some policyholders to pay supracompetitive prices so that others can pay less, require a labyrinth of regulations to enforce price restrictions, with adverse feedback effects on cost growth. That some states have practiced severe rate suppression for politically sensitive lines of business is irrefutable. By tending to reduce the financial strength of multistate insurers, those practices arguably have adverse spillovers on policyholders in other states.

Several state actions have responded to these problems. First, some states recently deregulated rates and policy forms for large commercial buyers, and others are considering that change. Second, some states modified their rate regulatory policy to produce a closer alignment of rates and costs over time and across consumers. Third, the NAIC is exploring model legislation to promote greater uniformity of agent licensing. Financial modernization legislation may hasten greater uniformity in that regard, including provisions for national licensing of agents if states fail to take action.

Solvency regulation is generally regarded as the raison d'être for insurance regulation. From an economic perspective, extensive rate regulation is unnecessary given the competitive structure of insurance markets. Periodic bouts of rate suppression in some states have made state regulation doubly vulnerable to criticism. State regulation is criticized for allegedly inefficient solvency regulation and for excelling at policies that distort prices inefficiently and impede well-functioning markets.

Summary. The modern history of insurance regulation is characterized by a notable dialectic. Following the manifestation of particular problems in insurance markets, pressure simultaneously increases for federal intervention and for states to take action to address the problems. Changes are made in state regulation, and the problems usually wane, without implying complete causality. Pressure for federal intervention likewise declines. Whether that system of federal and state competition is efficient is debatable.

Eroding Support for State Regulation

How has state insurance regulation remained preeminent in the face of dramatic growth in federal involvement in economic affairs in the twentieth century? There would appear to be at least two causes. First, insurance markets, in conjunction with state oversight, often perform reasonably, if not remarkably, well. Many states have economically sensible regulatory systems that focus attention on areas where the government can help achieve an orderly market, as opposed to taking actions that substantially undermine efficiency and redistribute wealth. The second cause is related. Although there have been exceptions earlier in this century, especially for life insurers, the insurance industry has traditionally supported state regulation.

Smaller insurers have been especially supportive of state regulation, maybe because they have to deal with fewer state insurance departments, or because domiciliary regulators protect them, perhaps in part by administrative red tape that hampers large, multistate insurers. Small property-liability insurers also might fear that federal regulation would be accompanied by the repeal of the industry's limited antitrust exemption. Some players, including insurance agents, probably have supported state regulation in part because it has historically been amenable to the separation of bank and insurance powers.

However, traditional industry support for state regulation has eroded in recent years for several reasons. Product evolution and increased competition at the national and international levels, including reduced reliance on cooperative pricing by property-liability insurers, have increased the costs of dealing with multiple state regulators and sharpened concerns over unnecessary duplication and conflicting state requirements. The narrowing of the industry's antitrust exemption by the courts and rate suppression in some states and time periods have weakened property-liability insurer support for the McCarran-Ferguson exemption. Many companies have begun to consider whether a partial or complete exemption from state rate regulation through some form of federal regulation might be in their interest, even if the antitrust exemption is further weakened or eliminated. In addition, continuing industry consolidation reduces the number of small, regional insurers that have tended to support state regulation. Court-sanctioned and legislative extensions of the authority of banking concerns to deal in insurance and recent changes in federal law dealing with financial services further weaken the traditional basis of support for state insurance regulation.

Partial Deregulation through Federal Regulation?

As noted above, the debate over insurance regulation is representative of the general debate over the relative advantages of centralizing or decentralizing government power. Observers like myself who favor decentralizing power (*Real Federalism;* see Michael Greve 1999) view state regulation more kindly than do those who favor a greater centralization of power in Washington. The strongest source of support for federal insurance regulation, however, is not philosophical. It is the desire by large segments of the insurance business for substantial deregulation in areas that have relatively little bearing on insolvency risk. That desire also undermines support for an interstate compact to achieve greater centralization of regulation. Creation of a compact would be less likely to produce material deregulation.

The case for substantial deregulation is compelling, both intellectually and empirically. Whether federal regulation would achieve appropriate deregulation is uncertain, but the need for deregulation *should* play a central role in the debate over who should regulate insurance. Until now there has been continued hairsplitting over the efficacy of the antitrust exemption and of state solvency regulation.

Some aspects of regulation are wealth-creating; they enhance the efficiency of the marketplace and thereby raise living standards. Other aspects destroy wealth, including the deadweight cost associated with many regulatory policies designed to redistribute income. Ignoring the latter tendency, reasonably good arguments can be made that greater centralization of insurance regulation could enhance efficiency. But we can only guess whether federal regulation would be less likely than state regulation to pursue material redistribution of wealth (for example, through widespread restrictions on risk classification).

Competition among the states helps discipline the tendency of insurance regulation to promote inefficient wealth transfers. State regulation allows insurers to "vote with their feet," admittedly at a substantial cost. Although insurer exit in the face of expropriation by regulation will generally be slow, the threat of exit is credible enough to provide some limits on inefficient regulatory behavior. Congress, federal agencies, and the federal courts have pursued many forms of inefficient income redistribution. The temptation to use insurance regulation to redistribute wealth will not necessarily be lower at the federal level or in a dual regulatory system, although international regulatory competition might discipline federal regulators to some extent.

The possibility also exists that federal solvency regulation might be accompanied by expanded protection of insurance buyers against loss from insurer insolvency. Such expansion in turn might materially undermine incentives for safety; that is, it might increase moral hazard, as was illustrated so vividly by the savings and loan crisis. A well-known argument for state regulation is that mistakes are localized. The frequency of regulatory failure may be greater in a decentralized state system, but the consequences are local and therefore much less severe.

Given the efficient-versus-inefficient regulation dichotomy, informed judgment on whether federal insurance regulation is in the public interest requires answers to at least three related questions:

- Would well-designed federal regulation be likely to produce material efficiencies, at least in part through appropriate deregulation?
- If so, will any politically achievable system of federal regulation likely be designed and implemented to achieve many of those efficiencies?
- If not, will any administrative efficiencies that are achieved outweigh the increased risk of a nationwide regulatory failure at some future date?

Notes

1. An appendix provides a brief overview of state regulation. See Robert Klein (1999) for details. The material in the appendix and my discussion of solvency experience draw from chapters 5 and 24 of my textbook with Greg Niehaus, *Risk Management and Insurance*. The historical overview draws from Robert I. Mehr and Emerson Cammack (1976) and benefits greatly from the collection edited by Spencer Kimball and Barbara Heaney (1995).

2. Section 4 of the act excepts federal labor law and the Merchant Marine Act from its application.

3. Many states have antitrust laws that apply to insurance.

4. See, for example, Kimball and Heaney (1995) for detailed discussion. My discussion here is intentionally cursory, as befits a nonlawyer writing for an audience that includes many persons who are not similarly blessed.

5. Assessments for life-health insurers prior to 1988 are net of any refunds for prior years' assessments during the year. The number of insolvencies was obtained from the NAIC. Property-liability assessments were obtained from the National Conference of Insurance Guaranty Funds; life-health assessments were obtained from National Organization of Life and Health Insurance Guaranty Associations. The assessment data are for new assessments during the year, except for life-health insurers prior to 1988, where the available data subtract any refunds during the year for assessments made in prior years that exceeded the amount ultimately needed to pay claims covered by the guaranty funds.

6. Assessments for Mutual Benefit Life totaled just $81 million.

7. Some evidence suggests that because of the rebound in high-yield bond prices that occurred in 1991, Executive Life might have been solvent if it could have survived until year-end. The corporation that succeeded Mutual Benefit Life and that was supervised by New Jersey regulators was in good enough financial shape to be offered for sale to the private sector in 1997.

References

Greve, Michael S. 1999. *Real Federalism*. Washington, D.C.: AEI Press.

Harrington, Scott E. 1991. "Should the Feds Regulate Insurance Company Solvency?" *Regulation: Cato Review of Business and Government* (Spring): 53–60.

———. 1992. "Policyholder Runs, Life Insurance Company Failures, and Insurance Solvency Regulation." *Regulation: Cato Review of Business and Government* (Spring): 27–37.

Harrington, Scott E., and Greg Niehaus. 1999. *Risk Management and Insurance.* Burr Ridge, Ill.: Irwin/McGraw Hill.

Kimball, Spencer L., and Barbara P. Heaney. 1995. *Federalism and Insurance Regulation.* Kansas City, Mo.: National Association of Insurance Commissioners.

Klein, Robert W. 1999. *A Regulator's Introduction to the Insurance Industry.* Kansas City, Mo.: National Association of Insurance Commissioners.

Macey, Jonathan R., and Geoffrey P. Miller. 1993. *Costly Policies: State Regulation and Antitrust Regulation in Insurance Markets.* Washington, D.C.: AEI Press.

Manders, John M., Therese M. Vaughan, and Robert H. Myers, Jr. 1994. "Insurance Regulation in the Public Interest: Where Do We Go from Here?" *Journal of Insurance Regulation* 12: 285–340.

Mehr, Robert I., and Emerson Cammack. 1976. "Regulation of the Insurance Business: Objectives, Methods and History." In *Principles of Insurance.* 6th ed. Homewood, Ill.: Richard D. Irwin.

Subcommittee on Oversight and Investigations of the Committee on Energy and Commerce, U.S. House of Representatives, Rep. John Dingell, chair. 1990. *Failed Promises—Insurance Company Insolvencies.* Report. Washington, D.C.: U.S. Government Printing Office.

Appendix
Overview of State Insurance Regulation

The insurance business is heavily regulated in the United States and most other developed countries. Each state has an insurance department (or commission) that implements state legislation governing the purchase and sale of insurance that is set forth in the state insurance code. In addition to specific mandates specified in the state's insurance code, the insurance department has the authority to establish rules and procedures to implement legislative directives. The state insurance commissioner is appointed by the governor in a significant majority of states and elected in the others.

When viewed broadly, insurance regulation includes the

TABLE 2–A
OVERVIEW OF REGULATED ACTIVITIES

Activity	Description	Principal Types of Coverage and Prevalence Across States
Licensing of insurers and agents / brokers	Granting, renewal, and revocation of license to conduct business by state insurance departments	All types of coverage and states
Insurer solvency	Solvency monitoring by state insurance departments, capital and financial reporting requirements, investment regulations, holding company regulation, guaranty funds	All types of coverage and states
Rates	Prior approval of rate changes and regulation of rate differentials across consumers by state insurance departments for the voluntary market	• Workers' compensation rates in about 80 percent of the states • Personal auto, homeowners, and other business property-liability insurance rates in about half of the states • Individual and small group health insurance in some states • Credit life and health insurance in some states

Residual markets	Industry must supply coverage through a residual market, such as an assigned risk plan or joint underwriting association, at a regulated rate to applicants who have difficulty obtaining it voluntarily	• Personal automobile in all states • Workers' compensation in all states • Urban and coastal property insurance in some states • Individual health insurance in some states
Content of policy forms	Regulation of contract language (including provisions governing cancellation and non-renewal) and approval of forms by state insurance departments	Most types of coverage in all states, except for most property-liability coverages sold to "large" businesses in about 20 states
Contract interpretation and enforcement	State insurance department enforcement of legislation dealing with market conduct and unfair trade practices	Most types of coverage in all states
Insurer sales practices and information disclosure	Regulation of sales practices through state insurance department enforcement of market conduct / unfair trade practices legislation; required disclosure of price information; production and dissemination of information about prices and quality by regulators.	Mainly for personal insurance in most states
Compulsory purchase of coverage (or minimum requirements for self-insurance)	Compulsory insurance laws and their enforcement by the states	• Personal auto liability in almost all states • Automobile personal injury protection coverage in most no-fault states • Workers' compensation insurance • Miscellaneous type of business and professional liability insurance in most states

SOURCE: Author.

state insurance code, its implementation by the state insurance department, and other legislation related to insurance (such as compulsory insurance requirements) governing the purchase, sale, or enforcement of insurance contracts. In addition to regulation, the courts have a significant effect on contractual relations between insurers and policyholders through interpretation and enforcement of contract provisions. The major regulated activities are summarized in table 2–A.

Insurance regulation is complex because of the scope of activities that are regulated and the differences in regulation across states. However, most major activities are regulated in most or all states using the same broad type of regulation, such as solvency regulation and regulation of policy forms. Additional uniformity, cooperation, and coordination of state insurance regulation are achieved by the activities of the National Association of Insurance Commissioners (NAIC). The NAIC is a voluntary organization of all state insurance commissioners that holds regular meetings to discuss insurance regulatory issues and develop model laws. (The precursor organization to the NAIC was established in 1871.)

Some coordination of state solvency regulation has been achieved by having the state insurance department in which the state is domiciled (chartered) play a leading role in certain aspects of solvency oversight, such as conducting and preparing reports based on on-site financial examinations. The NAIC plays a major role in promoting uniform financial reporting and risk-based capital requirements across states. In addition, the NAIC oversees the coordination of financial examinations of insurance companies by state regulators. As discussed in the main body of the chapter, in the early 1990s the NAIC developed risk-based capital requirements. It also established a solvency regulation accreditation program in 1991 that specifies minimum standards for state solvency regulation. States that adopt specified model laws related to solvency regulation and meet minimum standards for solvency monitoring are accredited by the NAIC. States that are not accredited face some risk of increased monitoring or regulation of their home (domestic) insurers by other states' insurance departments and of being known for weak regulation. Most states were accredited by 1999.

PART TWO

The Case for Federal Chartering and Regulation

3

Optional Federal Chartering for Property and Casualty Companies

Ernest T. Patrikis

To begin, I do not purport to speak for the property and casualty industry. In preparing these remarks, I have not consulted with any trade association or with any other firm.

My background is in banking, and if banking were regulated as insurance is regulated in the United States, loan agreements and interest rates would have to be approved by fifty state bank supervisors. It is awe-inspiring to think that something like that is actually done in the insurance industry, but clearly it raises the question of whether that is the best use of society's resources.

Banking law provides an interesting study for the question of whether optional federal chartering would be good policy. Banking involves both federal and state charters. Originally, except for the First and Second Banks of the United States, all banks were state-chartered, and after President Andrew Jackson refused to approve the rechartering of the Second Bank of the United States, all money—currency—was issued by state banks. The need to finance the Civil War resulted in the chartering of national banks, which were regarded as federal instrumentalities. To issue currency, national banks had to pledge U.S. government securities, thus financing the war effort. Similarly, savings and loans were authorized at the federal level to increase home ownership by making financing available, even though state-chartered S&Ls already existed.

That history is significant as we consider the decision to set up a system of federal chartering where a state system already exists. It requires a serious policy foundation. Whether such a foundation exists is the matter we are considering at this conference.

Again, if we look at banking we see an analogy. Now that banks can branch interstate, I think it is likely that more and more multi-state, state-chartered banks will convert to national charters. That is because there would be: (1) fewer bank supervisors to deal with on a daily basis, (2) fewer state laws and regulations with which to comply, and (3) economies of scale in advertising, administration, and compliance.

Should the pending financial modernization legislation become law, and should financial holding companies engage in insurance underwriting, then commercial bankers would not be pleased to find themselves dealing with fifty state insurance supervisors. They are likely to become another group pushing for change.

It is also useful to look at the evolution of regulation in the securities industry. Today, we see more and more federal preemption of state securities laws.

If the states were inclined to follow the path that the European Union has taken, I am not sure we would be meeting to address the need for a federal charter. Under the Insurance Directive, there is no form and rate regulation. An insurance company's home-state supervisor is its sole supervisor. No approval is needed to sell insurance across borders directly or to establish a branch in another country to sell insurance. That is the passport of the directive, and it is beginning to benefit the consumer. Auto insurance rates are beginning to come down in Germany as more out-of-state firms write policies there.

That is not to say that all is going as smoothly as it should. A host state can regulate for the public good, presumably to allow the host state to protect consumers. The European Commission has challenged several states that have not followed the directive, along with those states alleged to have exceeded regulation permitted for the public good.

How then can one find a solid rationale for the federal chartering and regulation of insurance? That can best be done by setting out some principles to be applied in evaluating proposals for federal chartering. The following is my first attempt at that effort. I have done it in the form of questions.

- Is there a need for a more cost-effective form of regulation?
- Is the underwriting business carried on in a uniform way across state borders?
- Will deregulation be fostered?
- Is there a need for more effective and efficient relations with other financial-organization supervisors and regulators in the United States, and with insurance and other financial-institution supervisors outside the United States?
- Is there a need to reduce the moral-hazard risk and systemic risk associated with state guaranty funds?
- Are some forms of insurance better suited for federal supervision and regulation than for state supervision and regulation?
- Is there a need for a comprehensive federal scheme replicating state schemes, or would a gradual transitional approach be more fruitful?

Where do I come out? I offer the following approach:

- There should be a federal-charter option for property and casualty business.
- That option should apply only to commercial business.
- That option should apply to something equivalent to the sophisticated-investor test in the federal securities laws or to coverage exceeding a certain dollar amount. In sum, the potential insured should be capable of negotiating on an equal footing with the insurer.
- There should be no form and rate regulation.
- There should be no federal guaranty fund.
- There should be a unique federal bankruptcy scheme for those insurance companies.
- The Federal Reserve Board should be the supervisor of those insurance companies.
- A company owning such an insurance company should be subject to comprehensive consolidated supervision by the Federal Reserve Board. That should include a source-of-strength policy.
- State laws should be preempted except to the extent that

they do not frustrate the efficient operation of those insurance companies. The Federal Reserve Board would have express authority to make those preemption determinations, subject to review by the courts of appeals.

We should recognize the efforts of the state insurance supervisors. The National Association of Insurance Commissioners deserves a great deal of credit for working toward harmonization of statutes, regulations, and rulings. Nonetheless, insurance-company staffs need to review state regulatory developments daily. We need to ascertain whether forms and premiums must be filed—a labor-intensive and time-consuming requirement.

Why have I selected the Fed as supervisor? There are several reasons. I believe that the Fed is well suited to the financial-stability type of supervision I have laid out. I believe that the Fed is best suited to serve as the overseer—not regulator or supervisor—of financial holding companies. The Reserve Banks already have a competent examination staff. The Fed also has excellent relationships with offshore supervisors. The Fed does not rely on appropriated funds and is a truly independent agency of the federal government.

That being said, however, the Tenth Amendment, states' rights, and the policy behind the McCarran-Ferguson Act cannot be ignored. State insurance departments are a source of employment and a part of the state power structure. Regulation and examination provide the state with income. In view of those considerations, I do not think that it is realistic or advisable to seek wholesale replication of insurance chartering, supervision, and regulation at the federal level. In addition, property and casualty companies will have a choice of a federal or a state charter. That narrow line of competition between federal and state insurance supervisors should lead to better supervisory policies and procedures.

I have long followed the guidance of one of my first-year law school professors: "Life by the yard is hard; life by the inch is a cinch." For that reason, I conclude that the narrow and focused proposal I have set out today is practical and feasible.

4
Optional Federal Chartering for Life Insurance Companies

Peter J. Wallison

The remarkable thing about the current interest in federal chartering for life insurance companies is that it does not arise out of a regulatory or financial crisis. As Scott Harrington's chapter makes clear, almost every serious past review of state-level insurance regulation sprang from a perceived or actual failure of some kind—either in the industry or by the state regulators. The initiative came from Congress, never from the industry itself.

This time, however, it appears that the impetus for looking at the question of federal chartering is coming from the industry. Although concern about the reaction of state regulators has caused individual insurance companies to keep their interest in federal chartering well hidden, those who follow insurance developments are aware of considerable interest and support within life industry councils—and serious study of legislative alternatives.

That sudden change of heart—from traditional opposition to cautious support—should come as no surprise. It is the result of competitive factors that we see all around us today. The likelihood that some members of the industry will openly support optional federal chartering becomes greater as the changes in competitive conditions become more pronounced.

In brief, the life industry has become interested in federal chartering and regulation because the competition it is facing today is cross-industry competition—head-to-head competition with banks and securities firms that appear to have competitive advantages arising out of their more flexible regulatory regimes. Although constitutional standards required state banking regulators long ago to develop a regulatory framework that permitted nationwide marketing of banking products—although not until recently did federal law authorize nationwide branching—the early decisions of the Supreme Court that treated insurance as subject only to state control resulted in a balkanized regulatory structure that seems wholly unsuited to the competitive environment of today.

In other words, when life insurance companies were once competing only with one another, no great competitive problems resulted from a fifty-state approval process for new products. All competitors were subject to the same impediments. But that level playing field is gone. Suddenly, the competitors that life insurers face are no longer equivalently burdened.

Today, life insurance companies are competing directly with banks and securities firms in two critical respects—each industry is offering similar products, and each is marketing nationally to the same customers.

Insurance products are beginning to have many of the characteristics of banking or securities products—and many banking and securities products have features that imitate or replicate insurance products. That convergence places considerable emphasis on the ability of a company quickly to develop and market a competitive product, but when a life insurer must get regulatory approval for a product from each of the fifty separate state markets in which it may be operating, that essential rapid response time is seriously attenuated.

The securities industry faces virtually no state-by-state product approval restrictions, and the banking industry has been able to address the product approval issue effectively through the option of federal chartering and regulation. But the life insurance industry remains frozen in time, the ward of a system in which approval for the nationwide rollout of a product requires approval by fifty state insurance regulators.

In addition to product competition, the life industry is also competing with banks and securities firms for the same customers and clients. That is not simply a case of the banks selling insurance; it is instead a reflection of the fact that insurance companies must now market themselves not simply as life insurers but as financial services firms. They must offer customers and clients not only straight insurance products but, among other things, financial advice, securities trading, investments, savings facilities, and funds transfer.

Thus, in addition to a convergence on products, there is also a convergence on customers. Banks, securities firms, and insurance companies are each vying to become the principal link between an individual or company and the financial markets.

Direct competition with the banking and securities industries has caused insurers, perhaps for the first time, to look closely at the regulatory regimes under which their competitors function. Although the comparatively light regime applicable to securities firms was well known, the regulatory advantages available to banks were impressive—especially since banks, as federally insured institutions, were supposed to be subject to especially stringent regulatory requirements.

From all appearances, however, the dual banking system—under which banks could choose whether to be chartered at the state or federal level—seemed to offer much greater flexibility and competitive opportunity for banks than insurance companies could easily recognize in their own regulatory regimes.

In addition, a structure in which insurance was regulated solely at the state level gave rise to other competitive disadvantages:

- First, as Scott Harrington notes in chapter 2, insurance has no spokesman at the federal level. When legislation is under consideration at the Treasury Department or at one of the banking agencies, and is brought to the councils of an administration for review, there is no one there to speak for the insurance industry. In my experience in government, that is certainly true.

To be sure, the Securities and Exchange Commission (SEC) does not necessarily advocate the positions of the securities industry, but at least it understands the industry's needs. And when an issue is being considered at the federal level that requires a detailed knowledge of the securities industry, it is possible to turn to someone from the SEC who can provide a fairly good idea of how proposed legislation might affect the securities industry, or how the industry is likely to react. There is no analogue at the federal level for insurance, and as a result, the industry must frequently play catch-up during the legislative process.

• Second, the insurance industry has seen banking's tremendous success in getting its products, its ideas, and its expansion approved by the Comptroller of the Currency at the national level, and then essentially forced on the states through federal preemption. The power inherent in federal preemption was probably not well understood when the national banking laws were drafted. To be sure, later court decisions enlarged the reach of the Comptroller's authority to preempt contrary state laws, but the ability of the Comptroller of the Currency to expand the scope of permissible activities for national banks—in turn requiring corresponding changes in state banking laws—is probably the single most important factor in giving the banks what the insurance industry regards as overwhelming regulatory advantages.

• Third, and of particular importance in evaluating the issue of optional federal chartering, is the effect of competition between federal and state regulators in creating a more accommodating regulatory environment for banks. Given what is now understood about the preemption power, it is unlikely that a federal insurance chartering agency will be given the same authority to preempt state law as the Comptroller of the Currency currently possesses. But the fact that each state will have to compete with a federal regulator to retain its complement of regulated entities immediately creates the prospect of more flexible and business-oriented state regimes. Somewhat paradoxically, the dual banking system has provided more flexibility than would a fifty-state regulatory system. That is largely because it is considerably easier for a bank to convert from a state charter to a federal charter, or vice versa, than it is for an insurance company to redomesticate out of the state in which it was originally chartered.

• Fourth, insurance companies are beginning to operate internationally, offering their products and making acquisitions overseas. In that activity they are discovering that state regulators do carry great weight in foreign countries. Foreign regulators, concerned about the safety and soundness of financial-services firms chartered elsewhere, are interested in knowing whether there is a responsible regulator in the home country of nondomestic insurance companies, banks, or securities firms that are operating within their borders. When the home country's safety-and-soundness regulator is a state regulator, foreign authorities may be reluctant to grant access to their markets, or to permit acquisitions of local businesses.

• Fifth, there is a widespread view among life insurers that they are subject to greater costs than their noninsurance competitors because they have to deal with fifty state regulators. In support of that proposition they would cite the need to have a compliance staff that is familiar with the laws and regulations in different states, and to make sure that all their agents, if they employ agents, are qualified under the laws of each state in which they operate. That can be an extremely expensive process, in addition to all the costs of filings for approval of products in each state in which those products may be offered. It seems obvious to the insurance industry that if there were only one place to go for an approval and one set of regulations to observe, such a regime must be much less expensive than the current system.

In chapter 8, Martin F. Grace and Robert W. Klein suggest that expense should not be a major consideration—that the costs of fifty state compliances are just not significant enough to support federal chartering and regulation. But at this time it remains an influential part of the case for optional federal chartering.

• Finally, the rapid development of the Internet and e-commerce as a means of attracting customers and selling financial services has exacerbated the deficiencies of the fifty-state regulatory structure for life insurers. E-commerce has two distinct characteristics—it is non-local, in the sense that a seller's website can be accessed from anywhere in the world, and it offers extraordinary opportunities for cross-selling. If a potential customer can be attracted to a website for one service, he or she can be given almost immediate access to another service at the click of a mouse button. A customer who has accessed a website to trade securities may become interested in a banking or insurance service, and if so, he or she can be presented with information or signed up for a trial or permanent arrangement on the spot. If an insurance product has not been approved in all states, the customer may have to be turned away; the benefits of non-locality and cross-selling are lost. In a competitive world where Internet marketing and cross-selling are major elements, the insurance industry's fifty-state regulatory regime may become an even more serious disadvantage.

PART THREE

The Case against Federal Chartering and Regulation

5

The Optional Federal Insurance Charter Is No Option At All

Robert B. Morgan

S ince 1945, the insurance industry in the United States has been regulated by the states under authority of the McCarran-Ferguson Act (hereinafter called "McCarran-Ferguson"). The principal objective of McCarran-Ferguson was to establish the primacy of the states in regulating the insurance industry. As section 1 of the act provides:

> Congress hereby declares that the continued regulation and taxation by the several States of the business of insurance is in the public interest, and that silence on the part of the Congress shall not be construed to impose any barrier to the regulation or taxation of such business by the several States.[1]

That principle is clarified in section 2 of the act:

> (a) State regulation. The business of insurance, and every person engaged therein, shall be subject to the laws of the several States which relate to the regulation or taxation of such business.[2]

Those time-honored principles are threatened by players who would like to experiment with the federal regulation of insurance and the concept of an optional federal insurance charter. No specific proposal for an optional federal charter is now before Congress, but some state-versus-federal regulation-of-insurance issues are being debated as Congress considers financial-services modernization legislation. The recent study by the American

Council of Life Insurance, comparing the costs of state and federal regulation, has also raised additional interest in the issue.

For those who support federal regulation or an optional federal insurance charter, it is easy to argue in favor of federal involvement, since the debate is mostly hypothetical. But when one compares any hypothetical federal system with the system of state regulation already in existence, the benefits of the state system for consumers and the industry far outweigh any perceived advantage of a federal system.

Consider the following:

Unique knowledge of the markets and local conditions. The states are the only logical choice for the comprehensive regulation of insurance. State regulators know the insurance markets within their borders. Although there are uniform national concerns in this industry as in many others, in uncountable ways insurance involves concerns of an intensely local nature. The concerns in Ohio, for example, with its multiple urban centers, lake-front communities, and manufacturing base, are quite different from the insurance issues raised in Iowa, with its thousands of farmers and few large urban areas.[3]

Flexibility. The attributes of an ideal regulatory insurance system include reasonableness, flexibility, adaptability to local markets, regulator skills, and the ability to spread the risk of bad regulation. Federal regulation cannot compete with state regulation in those areas.[4]

State regulation encourages innovation. State regulation encourages innovation. Companies often use a state as a laboratory for testing new product ideas before they are introduced on a national level.[5]

Less risk of regulatory mistakes. Under state regulation, good regulatory initiatives spread to other states and, conversely, the bad ideas tried in one state prevent others from making the same mistakes by offering real-market examples. Having fifty different regulators is less risky than gambling on a single federal regulator who might have an axe to grind against the insurance industry—and ultimate power over it.[6]

States have powerful incentives to do the job right. Individual states and their citizens bear the costs associated with regulating insurance providers, including the costs of any insolvencies that occur. State governments thus have a powerful incentive to do the job well, and the record shows they have done so.[7]

New federal bureaucracy. At a time when Congress is seriously considering empowering states in a myriad of areas, Congress should not strip the states of their authority to regulate in a business arena that has been within their virtually exclusive domain throughout this country's fruitful history.[8] The last thing America needs is another federal bureaucracy.

Experience and competency of regulators. Federal regulators lack the specialized experience and skills needed to regulate the insurance activities of insurance companies effectively.

Resources necessary to effectively and efficiently regulate. The federal government does not currently have the structures or regulations in place to get the job done. It would take a huge effort to duplicate the activity of the states in this regard. Consider these facts:

- In 1997, insurance products generated 3.2 million consumer inquiries and 392,000 actual complaints made to state regulators.[9]
- State insurance commissioners employ 10,000 regulatory personnel nationwide and spend $750 million annually to be the watchful eyes and helping hands on consumer insurance problems.[10]

The federal government is simply not equipped to take on such a role and develop a licensing and regulatory authority as sophisticated as a state system that has been 200 years in the making. To ensure effective consumer protection and consistent quality and dependability for the vast array of products now available in the insurance marketplace, state regulation should remain the only vehicle for protecting insurance consumers and regulating our good industry.

Consumer confusion. The option of a federal charter is no option at all, especially for consumers. Under an optional federal charter system, state-chartered insurers and federally chartered insurers would operate side by side in the states. Under those circumstances, consumer access to regulatory protection would become needlessly complicated by the mere existence of dual regulatory systems and the resulting confusion as to which system has jurisdiction over a particular consumer complaint. Protecting consumers during the sales process would be even more problematic, since state-regulated agents would be selling products offered by federally charted insurers, further complicating the question of which system has jurisdiction over a particular transaction. Insurance consumers should not have to roll the dice when deciding whom to contact for a problem.

The risk of a federal advocate. Some players argue that the insurance industry needs a federal regulator who will fight for our interests against other financial institutions and advocate our views before Congress, just as the Securities and Exchange Commission and the Office of the Comptroller of the Currency champion the securities and banking industries. But consider the other face of federal regulation, one that manifests itself at the Department of Housing and Urban Development: there, a single federal regulator with ultimate power over an industry might have an axe to grind against the industry. Alternatively, at the Internal Revenue Service the regulatory system itself becomes self-perpetuating and nonresponsive to the needs of those it regulates.[11]

Anticompetitiveness. Federal regulation will create an unlevel playing field between those insurers who opt for federal regulation and those whose insurance activities continue to be regulated by the states. With two completely separate and uncoordinated systems of regulation, there will be no uniformity among the forces and pressures that insurers face as a result of regulatory oversight. With separate and competing systems of rate and form regulation, underwriting requirements, market conduct regulation, insolvency requirements, and all other critical aspects of insurance regulation, another unnatural force will enter the insurance marketplace: choice of regulatory scheme (state or federal). That will result in an unfair and anticompetitive distribution of market advantages and disadvantages based on choice of regulatory system, and it will destroy the level playing field on which our industry now competes.

State regulation is not without imperfections. Although state regulation is by no means without imperfections (for example, countersignature laws and lack of uniform agent licensing laws), individual state regulators and the National Association of Insurance Commissioners are working hard to further enhance state regulation. By continuing the efforts already underway to standardize regulation among the states, state regulation will be further strengthened for the benefit of consumers and the industry.

Conclusion

Consumers clearly have an enormous financial and emotional stake in ensuring that the promises made by insurance providers are kept. Collectively, the insurance premiums paid by American consumers in 1997 amounted to $116 billion for auto coverage, $29 billion for homeowners' policies, $107 billion for life insurance, and $216 billion for health coverage. Almost half a trillion dollars goes toward buying annual personal insurance coverage, a unique product that is purchased to protect people during the times in their lives when they are most vulnerable.[12]

Given the sophisticated insurance licensing and regulatory structure developed exclusively at the state level over the past 200 years, and given the current climate disfavoring the creation of more federal regulatory authority (especially when it is duplicative of current state efforts), reaffirmation of the rights of states to regulate the insurance business appears to be the only viable solution. Such reaffirmation is required to ensure that all entities involved in the insurance industry are on a level playing field; to ensure that they are all subject to effective consumer protection requirements; and to ensure that the insurance-buying public has consistent assurances of quality.[13]

Notes

1. McCarran-Ferguson Act, ch. 20, §1, 59 Stat. 33 (1945) (current version at 15 U.S.C. §1011).

2. McCarran-Ferguson Act, ch. 20, § 2, 59 Stat. 34 (1945) (current version at 15 U.S.C. §1012).

3. *See Hearings on H.R. 10 Before the Subcomm. on Finance and Hazardous Materials of the House Comm. on Commerce*, 106th Congress, 1st Sess. (May 5, 1999) (statement of Scott A. Sinder, Partner, Baker & Hostetler, LLP, on behalf of Independent Insurance Agents of

America, National Association of Life Underwriters, and National Associate of Professional Insurance Agents) [hereinafter cited as *H.R. 10 Hearings* (Sinder Statement)].

4. *See* Ramirez, "No Studies Needed to Confirm That States Beat Fed Regulation," *National Underwriter* (April 12, 1999): 59.

5. Ibid.

6. Ibid.

7. *See Hearings on H.R. 10 Before the Subcomm. on Finance and Hazardous Materials of the House Comm. on Commerce*, 106th Congress, 1st Sess. (May 5, 1999) (statement of George Nichols, III, Commissioner of Insurance of Kentucky, on behalf of National Association of Insurance Commissioners) [hereinafter cited as *H.R. 10 Hearings* (Nichols Statement)].

8. *See H.R. 10 Hearings* (Sinder Statement), *supra* note 3.

9. *See H.R. 10 Hearings* (Nichols Statement), *supra* note 7.

10. Ibid.

11. *See* Ramirez, *supra* note 4.

12. *See H.R. 10 Hearings* (Nichols Statement), *supra* note 7.

13. *See H.R. 10 Hearings* (Sinder Statement), *supra* note 3.

6

Why the Dogs Are Not Barking

Jack R. Wahlquist

Much of the prevailing discussion of federal chartering of insurance companies can be characterized as skirmishes in a series of overlapping turf wars. Although it is natural to expect turf wars, we desperately need careful and dispassionate analysis to come to grips with those issues.

I would like to issue one disclaimer and submit one confession. These are my personal views only and do not reflect those of any company, association, or organization. I certainly do not represent a mythical "insurance industry position." Indeed, at this time there is none. There are efforts to develop a consensus concerning regulatory reform, but it is immensely premature to try to divine what that might be.

My confession is that I do not really intend to make the case against dual regulation. Doing so could imply a defense of the status quo, which I believe is indefensible. Emphatically, I have not given up on state regulation. But for the current system of state regulation to survive, it must be dramatically and substantially reformed. The nature of that reform could be the subject of another conference, but it lurks in the background theme of this volume.

The absence of reform results in the insurance industry's "sounds of silence"—or, to segue from Paul Simon to Sir Arthur Conan Doyle's "Silver Blaze," the reason why the dogs are not barking in the night. Perhaps a consideration of why the life insurance dogs are not barking will provide some insights into the dynamics of the policy options.

Our Industry Isn't an Industry Anymore

The insurance industry, with its well-defined subsets of property and casualty, life, and health, is being transformed before our eyes. We are developing into a financial-services industry, the exact shape and dimensions of which are at times only hazily recognizable. What used to be industry subsets now seem more like product lines in the new industry.

We can reasonably expect that the uncertainty about the validity, dimensions, and velocity of the shift of industry paradigm will dampen some executives' ardor for an emphatic and public determination as to the form of future regulation. Moreover, the characteristics of a system designed to provide proper regulation are probably substantially different from what we have today. One reason the dogs are not barking is that they are trying to figure out where their kennels are going to be located.

Where Have All the Actuaries and Lawyers Gone?

The professions of law and actuarial science, together with marketing and insurance investment management, were formerly the likeliest career paths to life-insurance-company management. Now, commercial banking, investment banking, and even academia are the paths to the CEO suite of increasing numbers of life insurers. The remarkable transition might be attributed in one degree or another to (1) the industry paradigm shift noted above, (2) an abject failure of the insurance industry to develop and retain adequate successor management, or (3) in some cases, a patient *in extremis* hoping for a miracle cure.

In short, many more bankers are running insurance companies than insurance executives are running banks. Compounding that development is the large and growing number of insurers owned by international financial institutions. Those trends mean that many key policymakers have not been raised in a tradition of state regulation and do not necessarily have doctrinal loyalty to its preservation. Even more important, they have direct experience with other forms of regulation (including dual regulation and self-regulatory organizations), and consequently they have ready benchmarks for evaluating competing regulatory systems. That personal dynamic is significant and should not be overlooked or underemphasized.

Is the Agent Still King?

I knowingly tread on dangerous ground here. By way of preface, I am a sincere believer that insurance is sold, not bought, and that the American agency system has historically been the most effective way of distributing the life insurance product.

Formerly, it was a commonplace in traditional life insurance companies that the Agent (always capitalized) is King. On a slightly more elevated plane, interminable debates have questioned whether the real customer was the Agent or rather what computer people would call the "end user"—an infelicitous expression for a purchaser of life insurance. Those debates are generally over; a customer is a customer, and the organization must be organized to serve that customer. In some companies there remains an absolute and unshakable commitment to the agency system of distribution. In many companies, though, that is only one of several alternative distribution systems. And there are many successful life insurers who do not use that form of distribution at all. Increasingly, the choice of distribution systems is an economic rather than a theoretical one.

How does all that affect the choice of regulatory policy? In two ways. First, there has been a well-documented decrease in the absolute numbers of licensed agents. Agents remain a powerful political force, and their influence should in no way be discounted. But sheer numbers may conceal the fact that, increasingly, those agents are also licensed under competing regulatory systems, and they too have ready benchmarks for evaluating the relative merits of those systems. Significantly more insurance agents are living in legislative and congressional districts than there are life insurance companies domiciled there. But the calculus of political influence may be changing, and that change may help to drive the determination of policy. Second, and perhaps more important, the significant number of insurance companies that do not rely on the traditional distribution system could well mean that, in the formulation of regulatory policy, those companies will not be significantly influenced by agent concerns.

The Impact of Creeping Federal Regulation

Most observers would say that we currently have a system of state regulation of insurance. That's not really the case. Beginning with Employee Retirement Income Security Act's (ERISA) preemption of regulation of employee welfare plans, we have had the Health Care Financing Administration's (HCFA) mandate of Long-Term Care Product Design, the Comprehensive Omnibus Budget Reconciliation Act's (COBRA) provisions for extension of benefits, and the Kennedy-Kassebaum portability mandates. I am sure that I have missed some. Now pending are provisions relating to genetic testing and privacy—particularly of medical records.

Narrowly focused interest groups are now looking for federal solutions, either bypassing or overriding state legislation and regulation. Members of Congress are *not* deciding that those issues are the province of state regulation, and they are *not* abstaining from consideration. Many in the insurance industry see those legislative vehicles as a means to bring order to a chaotic melange of sometimes conflicting state actions.

That insidious approach to a patchwork system of shared regulation, unfettered by serious regulatory policy discussion, is probably the worst of all possible alternatives.

Ignorance of Colbert's Law (and Its Regulatory Corollaries) Is No Excuse!

It was reputedly Louis XIV's tax collector Jean-Baptiste Colbert who decreed, "The Art of Taxation is so plucking the goose as to obtain the largest amount of feathers with the least amount of hissing." The regulatory corollary obviously depends on regulating stringently enough but not so stringently as to lose at least the grudging support of the industry to be regulated. It is certainly not my intention to suggest that the regulators should be the captives of the industry. Perhaps it is more accurate to suggest that there has to be an underlying respect and confidence on the part of those regulated in the capability and efficiency of the regulatory system. My own personal judgment is that the level of respect and confidence has sustained a substantial and continuing erosion that is likely to affect the dynamic of regulatory policy.

The increased volume and amplitude of insurance industry hissing seems to have occurred in both negative and positive contexts. Or perhaps it is more useful to think in terms of sins of commission and omission.

The perception of sins of commission is directed toward the operational effectiveness of the individual state regulatory agencies and to the more strategic, quasi-legislative functioning of the National Association of Insurance Commissioners (NAIC). When executives are constantly being directed by the marketplace to think globally and to respond quickly, many in the insurance industry find it increasingly frustrating to deal with those who lack understanding of the national scope of operation, and who measure progress in light years. A few examples of perceived failures that are driving this evaluation include: the painfully slow process of policy-form approval, with its resulting impact on competitive advantage over other insurance and alternative noninsurance products; the mire to be navigated in securing approval for multijurisdictional operations; the intransigent extraterritoriality of at least one regulatory agency; and the speed of the response to multistate agent-licensing issues.

At the strategic level, the evolution of the NAIC from a voluntary association of those seeking a means of communication with their colleagues to an entity attempting to overlay a national regulatory system over a state system has certainly not been an unqualified success. The difficulties of coping with the fits and starts of that process have eroded industry support.

But those complaints are not new; they are enduring, and they may only be driving attitudes at the margin. It is the developing sense of sins of omission that have the most impact on those in the insurance industry. There is a palpable feeling, particularly among those who have been directly involved in the process of financial-services reform, that although other industry regulators may "woodshed" their constituents, they champion the interests of their own industry. The Federal Reserve Board and the Treasury are vigorous regulators, but they are equally champions of a sound, growing, strong, and prosperous banking industry; the Securities and Exchange Commission is equally vigilant in advocating the interests of the securities industry.

Who Advocates the Insurance Industry?

The consensus is that no one does. Further, that failure of advocacy is generally viewed as a competitive disadvantage that insurance companies suffer, to the advantage of their financial-services competitors.

I have written above that, with respect to financial-services reform, the current regulatory system has failed to grasp the essentially symbiotic relationship between the insurance regulators and the insurance industry. Lest you are misled into thinking that is an aberration, consider the problems outlined below.

Taxing Deferred Acquisition Costs. The Omnibus Budget Reconciliation Act of 1990 (OBRA) rejected (for federal income tax purposes) some of the vital principles of state regulatory accounting. Negating the conservative regulatory requirement that acquisition expenses be recognized immediately, OBRA ostensibly required that they be capitalized and amortized over a period of years. The effect was to deny a current deduction for the unamortized portion of the acquisition expenses that are required to be immediately expensed for statutory accounting purposes. I have deliberately said "ostensibly required" because that provision amounted to a thinly disguised premium tax—one that had previously been expressly reserved as a source of revenue to the states.

The impact on the insurers was twofold. First, there was a disjunction between required statutory accounting and federal taxation. That is not a theoretical construct. While companies were trying to preserve capital for increasingly stringent regulatory purposes, they were penalized by increased taxes. The resulting higher cost of supporting those capital requirements placed the life insurers at a competitive disadvantage with other providers of financial services. Second, the burden of an extra tier of premium taxes (even giving effect to the later partial amortization of the remainder of the capitalized acquisition expenses) increased the competitive disadvantage of insurance products vis-à-vis other financial-services products.

From the regulatory point of view, the challenges were again twofold. The federal government rejected one of the basic principles of statutory accounting and consequently of solvency regulation. And, probably more important, the federal government mounted a not-so-subtly-disguised attack on the revenue base hitherto preserved to the states—the premium flow of insurance companies.

One would expect that such a blatant attack on two bedrock elements of state regulation would provoke a spirited and sustained defense by the state regulatory system. One would also expect that more recent sustained attempts to expand the burden of that tax would invite continued defense. To my knowledge, there has been no such defense of the states' regulatory position.

Class Action Lawsuits. It is not my purpose to defend any abuse of the insurance consumer. Fraudulent market practices must be forcefully identified, investigated, and prosecuted. However, class action and other lawsuits over recent years deserve close attention and analysis. Parenthetically, it should be noted that a class action lawsuit against a mutual company (as most of these announced suits were) really amounts to awarding funds—if any, after legal expenses—to one class of policy owners (the plaintiffs) from another class of policy owners (the remaining owners of the mutual enterprise). The regulators' exercise of jurisdiction to ascertain the propriety of this reallocation has escaped my notice.

Of graver import were the fairly well reported facts that groups of attorneys sponsored meetings to act in concert to identify insurers as targets of litigation; that they acted in concert to coordinate litigation threatening the solvency of the target insurers; that they advertised to find nominal plaintiffs to be parties to litigation; and that they entered into settlements seriously affecting the capital and surplus of licensed insurers.

Certainly, I am not aware of the facts of each individual case, and perhaps justice was served in each and every one of them. But I am unaware of any state regulator's expressed public concern about that massive attempt to reallocate funds dedicated to the solvency of the regulated insurers. One wonders whether, had the phrase "Wall Street speculators," or "Middle Eastern financial terrorists," or "drug lords" been substituted for the more user-friendly "consumer activists" or "class action specialists," the regulatory apparatus would have been supine.

The litany of factors that, to one degree or another, may well be contributing to a significant change in attitude should not be interpreted as negatively writing off the prospects for continued state regulation. One tends to be most critical of those for whom one has the most affection and respect. But those opinions indicate that the deafening silence of the not-barking dog should be a source of gravest concern to the state regulatory system. The best argument against a system of dual regulation is a dramatic and substantial reform of the current system of state regulation. The impetus for that reform must come from the state regulatory system itself. If that initiative does in fact come to pass, I am confident that the life insurance industry will again become united in defending the defendable.

7
The Views of the National Association of Insurance Commissioners

Remarks by Jack Chesson

I have always worked in insurance from the public policy perspective. Too often, industry people forget that insurance is rooted in public policy.

Nobody buys insurance because they want to or like to. It's almost as exciting as buying tires for a car. We do it because we have to. Many times, we have to because somebody else tells us to—when we get a mortgage, or when we buy a car, for example.

Nor are insurance companies popular with the public. That is because insurance is fundamentally different from banking or other federally regulated industries, such as securities. Insurance is a very complicated commercial product; a bank statement is one page long. It is very clear what we owe the bank, what the bank owes us, and how much interest we have earned. An auto insurance policy, by contrast, is extremely complicated.

For that reason, insurance is regulated for the benefit of policyholders and consumers, not only to protect them against the difficulty of understanding insurance contracts but also to ensure that the insurance company itself is solvent. Insurance companies must be solvent, because the most basic consumer right is to get the claim paid. After all, insurance is purchased to pay for those events that life presents us, many of them unhappy.

Considering the question of federal versus state chartering, a number of the contributors to this volume express ideas with which I agree. The states have the existing resources already in place. They spend $750 million a year; they have 10,000 people; they have established agencies. That system, which is working today, will be eroded if the federal government moves in.

In addition, no one should assume that setting up a federal regulatory system for insurance will be politically easy. For one thing, state governors will be very concerned about the loss of tax revenue that will accompany the loss of regulated insurance companies to the federal government.

And there also remains the question of where to locate the insurance regulator within the federal government. That is the tough nut that was not cracked during the time the Dingell bill was under consideration, nor the Brooke bill before it.

It is first of all a problem of congressional committee jurisdiction. The Commerce Committee would clearly think itself entitled to jurisdiction over an insurance regulator, and that is where jurisdiction would likely be lodged. But in that case the regulation would have to be performed by an agency, or by part of an agency under the jurisdiction of the Commerce Committee.

The Federal Trade Commission would not be appropriate, nor would the Commerce Department, which is largely a promotional agency and not in the regulatory business.

The Securities and Exchange Commission (SEC) would be a good candidate from the Commerce Committee's perspective, simply because people know it and trust it. But the SEC believes it has its hands full dealing with securities matters—its real function—and would roundly resist taking on more responsibilities.

The bank regulators would not be suitable, in part because they are overseen by the Banking Committee. Furthermore, as we know from the savings and loan experience, where the banking regulators had jurisdiction, the regulators had no trouble subordinating regulation and disclosure to their primary function of protecting the banks. That means that they did not disclose the things that were causing the S&Ls to go bankrupt—as securities laws would require them to do. They kept those facts secret, in order to preserve what they thought was the safety of the banks they were regulating. And we would always have that problem.

Finally, there is the National Association of Insurance Commissioners (NAIC). We all know a lot about the NAIC. When I first came to work there, one of the old hands asked me, "Do you know what 'NAIC' stands for?" I was fairly naïve, and responded, "No, what?" He replied, "No Action Is Contemplated."

"Well," I said, "we ought to have a new regime here." The NAIC really started doing something, and we told people, "This is not your father's NAIC." We have new leaders, new people, a new mandate. The NAIC is currently active in the H.R. 10 debate. The commissioners have personally come to Washington, and I see a lot of good regulators. I see a lot of dedication and a lot of people who understand the problems this volume addresses.

They are pushing for uniformity and efficiency. They understand that they have to work with the federal government to get better regulation. In the past, that sentiment was anathema; now, the leaders and all the members of the NAIC have agreed that they want to cooperate with the government, and the NAIC will seek support for any amendments we can elicit from the federal government, to give the NAIC the tools it needs to get the job done.

Finally, we are working on a federal-state partnership. That is the reality. It should always have been the reality; regulators of all stripes should work together. We have been actively working with the regulators at the federal agencies to create regulatory cooperation agreements.

With all the new activity at the state level, it is unlikely that the state responsibility can be taken away. That is especially true in light of the issues and concerns that have now taken center stage. Remember that insurance ultimately is for the benefit of policyholders and consumers. Solvency was the key issue in the debate ten years ago, but I think that consumer protection is going to be the key to the new debate.

When people have consumer complaints, calling the federal government will not be satisfactory. People will want to speak with their state insurance department, not their Congress member or some remote federal agency.

I believe that the state system is coming around. State insurance commissioners are doing things that need to be done. For all the faults of the state system, it is there. It works well in many, many ways and it is improving.

In light of those realities, is anyone really going to say, "Let's take a leap into the unknown of federal regulation"? I don't think so.

PART FOUR

Are There Cost Savings in Federal Chartering?

8

Efficiency Implications of Alternative Regulatory Structures for Insurance

Martin F. Grace and
Robert W. Klein

T he insurance industry is undergoing an unprecedented evolution in terms of the structure of its markets, its products and services, and its scope of operations and transactions. That evolution is being spurred by the integration of financial-services markets and global competition, along with other economic, demographic, and technological forces. Those developments are renewing a long-standing discussion of the framework for insurance regulation in the United States.

Introductory Context

Insurance regulation in the United States is somewhat unique with respect to its reliance on the states as the primary locus of regulatory authority.[1] The states regulate many areas of intrastate commerce, but their regulation of insurance is peculiar given the interstate operations of many insurers. In contrast, the federal government has a substantial role in the regulation of other financial services, with state authority generally limited to

This chapter presents a preliminary discussion of the efficiency implications of alternative regulatory structures for insurance. Scott Harrington provided helpful comments on an earlier version of this chapter. Any remaining errors or omissions are the responsibility of the authors.

institutions and transactions confined within state boundaries. The increasing competition between various financial institutions and the potential reduction in legal barriers between banking and insurance activities prompts a comparison of their regulatory structures. Some might argue that consumers would be better served if insurers were regulated more like banks, with optional federal chartering and regulation of insurance companies.

One of the issues raised by such a proposal is the relative efficiency of alternative regulatory structures for insurance. Does regulation by the states impose extra costs or inefficiencies that could be avoided through federal regulation? How should regulatory costs be defined and measured? Does one assess state insurance regulation as it is, or optimally configured? What is the alternative structure by which the efficiency of state regulation should be judged? Would optional federal chartering or other structural changes facilitate reforms in insurance regulatory policies that would enhance market efficiency?

Overview of Chapter

This chapter initiates an inquiry into the relative efficiency of state insurance regulation and related issues.[2] We lay a foundation for our analysis by reviewing the reasons why insurance needs to be regulated and distinguishing what we consider to be essential regulatory functions from others that the states have chosen to perform. That distinction is important in determining costs inherent to a state regulatory structure and the potential benefits of regulatory reforms. We then compare the current institutional structures of insurance regulation and banking regulation. We postulate an optional federal charter/regulation system for insurance as our basis for assessing the relative costs of a state-based regulatory system. Our review includes the role of the National Association of Insurance Commissioners (NAIC), which helps to coordinate state insurance regulatory activities and provides support services to the states.

That material is followed by a discussion of the types of costs pertinent to insurance regulation and issues associated with their measurement. We identify three basic categories of costs: (1) government expenditures on regulation; (2) direct or tangible costs incurred by entities in complying with regulation; and (3) indirect or intangible costs reflecting market distortions caused by regulation, net of any benefits derived from regulation. As one moves down that list of costs, they become increasingly difficult to quantify and compare. We confine our quantitative analysis to direct regulatory expenditures and estimates of compliance costs. We assess other costs in qualitative terms. While intangible costs are the most difficult to measure, they may also be the most significant.

An important issue is the scope and design of regulatory policies and their implications for regulatory costs and market efficiency. There are different perspectives on whether reforms of regulatory policies would be more or less likely with increased federal involvement in insurance regulation. The resolution of such a question is beyond the scope of this chapter, but we recognize its importance and comment on it.

Our estimates of regulatory compliance costs are based on a multiple regression analysis of insurer expenses. We look at the relationship between various expense ratios and two possible indicators of compliance costs: the amount of business written in a restrictive regulatory environment and the number of states or lines in which an insurer conducts business. We examine the relationship between those explanatory variables and the ratio of total expenses to premiums, salary expenses to premiums, claims costs to premiums, and the ratio of regulatory license fees to total premiums. We control for other factors affecting insurer expenses, such as its volume of business, lines of business, and type of distribution system.

Our hypothesis is that regulation imposes compliance costs and that firms operating in restrictive regulatory environments or in more states are likely to have higher compliance costs. Our results are consistent with that hypothesis, as the amount of business written in restrictive environments is positively related to higher expense ratios (especially for life insurance companies), as is the number of states in which an insurer conducts business.

We conclude that the potential savings from optional federal chartering depend greatly on the scope and policies of federal regulation and how they would differ from the state regulatory system that may evolve in the future. We believe that there would be some savings from federal regulation, probably small, in the area of solvency or financial oversight. Much larger potential savings could be achieved from delegating current market regulatory functions to a federal entity. Alternatively, significant efficiencies could be achieved under the current state system or an alternative federal-state system by eliminating nonessential market regulations and standardizing those regulations that are retained.

It is important to stress that this chapter represents a first step in assessing the efficiency of our state-based system of insurance regulation and the advantages and disadvantages of alternative institutional structures and regulatory policies. Estimating regulatory costs is a formidable task, and we need to do much more work in this area. We also did not examine the regulatory costs imposed on insurance intermediaries—that is, agents and brokers. Further, the issue of relative costs is only one of a broader set of issues involved in the debate about how insurance should be regulated. That is a debate that will likely continue for some time and engender much more research. Our hope is that this chapter contributes to a thoughtful policy discussion of the structure and scope of insurance regulation.

Regulatory Objectives

Our discussion of the structure of insurance regulation begins with a review of the essential objectives of regulation. It is important to consider the functions that regulators need to perform and to compare those with the functions they do perform. Economic theory provides a basis for identifying essential regulatory objectives and functions. Arguably, the current scope of insurance regulation extends beyond that which benefits consumers. Confining state regulatory efforts to critical areas could reduce costs and improve outcomes without any changes in the institutional structure of state insurance regulation. Further efficiencies might be achieved by improving regulatory policies and procedures in critical areas without altering the role and authority of the states. Alternatively, optional federal chartering or other structural changes could promote better regulatory policies.

Why Should We Regulate Insurance? Regulation is best suited to remedy certain market failures and not necessarily market problems (for example, high prices) caused by other external forces, such as escalating claims costs. Market failures constitute violations of the structural conditions for workable competition, which include entry and exit barriers, firm market power, externalities, and information constraints. The purpose of regulation should be to correct market failures, or at least to minimize their negative effects, and to improve allocative efficiency (Spulber 1989).

Not all market failures, however, are amenable to regulatory remedies. Hence, the criteria for regulating a certain activity could be stated as follows: (1) Is there a significant market failure with substantial adverse effects on consumers or society? (2) Can regulation significantly improve market performance? There are two types of failures afflicting insurance markets that regulation might help to correct: information problems and principal-agent conflicts.

Information Problems. Insurers and consumers need information to make good decisions about insurance transactions. The implications of asymmetric information for insurers—adverse selection and moral hazard—are well documented (Varian 1992). Insurers seek to minimize those problems through contract provisions, risk classification and selection, and pricing. Information is costly and these mechanisms are imperfect, but insurers have been able to develop viable private markets for many risks.

Insurance buyers also face problems in acquiring the information they need, and individual consumers appear to be less able or less willing to overcome those problems without regulatory assistance (Joskow 1973; Schlesinger 1998). Consumers need information with respect to prices, the meaning of insurance contract provisions, the quality of service offered by different insurers, and the financial strength of insurers and their ability to meet their contractual obligations. It is costly for consumers to acquire that information, and the smaller the buyer, the fewer the resources that buyer can afford to expend on information acquisition. Further, it is apparent that some consumers choose to remain uninformed and myopic, regardless of their resources or the costs and benefits of acquiring information. Uninformed consumers are likely to make suboptimal decisions about insurance, which not only hurt them but, in some instances, could have adverse effects on other consumers or on the general public.[3] Hence, it can be argued that there are net benefits to imposing certain regulatory restrictions on insurers and insurance transactions to avoid particularly bad consumer decisions stemming from ignorance.

Principal-Agent Conflicts. Principal-agent conflicts arise because of the differing incentives of principals and agents and because of the principal's problem in monitoring and controlling the behavior of his agent. In an insurance contract, the insured could be viewed as the principal and the insurer as his agent. The insurer seeks to maximize profits and the value of the company; the consumer seeks to maximize the risk protection and benefits received under their contract. The insured pays a premium and the insurer holds funds to pay claims contingent on their contract. However, the insurer could refuse to honor its obligations or to take on additional financial risk that would jeopardize its ability to meet its obligations. Insureds can try to monitor their insurer's behavior and take legal action if necessary to protect their interests, but that is costly and possibly beyond the capacity of many smaller insureds. In a legal dispute, an insurer may have substantially more resources and bargaining power than a small policyholder has. Hence, it can be argued that regulators can assist consumers by weighing in on their side to ensure that insurers meet their contractual obligations.

Social and Political Objectives. Voters and legislators may prefer insurance market outcomes that differ from those that would result from competitive market forces. For example, voters may favor compulsory auto liability insurance and regulatory limits on the rates paid by high-risk drivers. The feasibility and social welfare gains from such policies are debatable, but they are present in all states to varying degrees. The costs of enforcing politically driven regulations at the state level could be very high. The magnitude of those costs could differ substantially under a federal system. A realistic assessment of regulatory costs should consider the possible continuation of regulations motivated by social and political preferences. Indeed, federal insurance regulation could be more restrictive than the current state system in response to interest-group pressures. The congressional appetite for restrictions on health insurers suggests that that kind of regulation would not be precluded under a federal system. Some might believe, however, that optional federal chartering would discourage attempts by regulators to transfer wealth.

What Do We Need to Regulate?

The existence of insurance market failures attributable to information costs and principal-agent conflicts can result in suboptimal consumer decisions, excessive insolvency risk, and abusive market practices. Regulation can ameliorate those market failures and the inefficiencies they cause. At the same time, it is not obvious that regulation can or should try to fix all the problems that may arise from those or other alleged insurance market flaws. Furthermore, the costs imposed by regulatory restrictions have to be balanced against any perceived benefits. Below, we discuss two areas of insurance regulation where government intervention seems to have fairly broad acceptance as well as a plausible economic foundation.

Limiting Financial Risk. The public interest argument for the regulation of insurer solvency derives from inefficiencies created by costly information and principal-agent problems (Munch and Smallwood 1981). Insurance company owners have diminished incentives to maintain a high level of safety to the extent that their personal assets are not at risk for unfunded obligations to policyholders that would arise from insolvency.[4] It is costly for consumers to properly assess an insurer's financial strength in relation to its prices and quality of service. Insurers also can increase their corporate risk profile after policyholders have purchased a policy and paid premiums.

Thus, in the absence of regulation, imperfect consumer information and principal-agent problems would result in an excessive number of insolvencies.[5] That does not mean that most insurers would fail without regulation, but regulation can constrain the behavior of insurers that might otherwise sustain an unacceptably high probability of ruin, and regulators may be able to accomplish that at a lower cost than the market can. Regulatory requirements on financial reporting and disclosure also may enhance the transparency of insurance transactions. Solvency regulation can help to limit insurers' insolvency risk and to decrease insolvency costs in accordance with policyholders' preference for safety. The need for regulation of institutions with fiduciary responsibilities is generally accepted.

There are different views on how insurance financial regulation should be conducted. It is generally accepted that a sound financial regulatory system entails appropriate "solvency margins," effective monitoring of insurers' financial condition, and timely intervention against high-risk or troubled insurers. Beyond those basic elements, financial regulatory systems vary significantly among countries (Skipper 1998). In the United States, the states have employed a "prescriptive" approach to financial regulation, under which insurers must comply with a detailed set of restrictions on their financial structures and transactions. Alternatively, the United Kingdom and many European countries follow a "prudential" regulatory philosophy. That approach provides insurers greater flexibility, which is compensated by stricter entry requirements, more intensive regulatory monitoring, and greater regulatory discretion in intervening against insurers.

As in other jurisdictions, state regulators in the United States utilize their control of insurers' entry into their markets and authorization to conduct business as their principal tool to coerce insurers to comply with regulations. State statutes set forth the requirements for incorporation and licensing to sell insurance, and as a result, an insurer must obtain a license in every state in which it does business.[6] State statutes require insurers to meet certain minimum-capital and surplus standards and financial reporting requirements, and to authorize regulators to examine insurers and take other actions to protect policyholders' interests. The states have established fixed minimum capital requirements, as well as risk-based capital requirements (based on a common formula developed by the National Association of Insurance Commissioners [NAIC]).

If an insurer fails to comply with a state's regulations, regulators can deny or revoke the insurer's license to do business. An insurer's state of domicile also can place the insurer into receivership, with court approval, if it is in hazardous condition. As a matter of practice, the domiciliary state is an insurer's principal financial regulator, but other states in which an insurer does business also monitor its financial condition and can take action against it if necessary.

The states perform the following functions to meet financial regulation objectives:

- processing applications for admission;
- reviewing mandatory annual and quarterly financial statements and other reports;
- performing financial analysis and conducting early warning tests;
- conducting periodic and targeted financial examinations;
- engaging in informal and formal interventions against troubled insurers;
- administering receiverships;
- overseeing insolvency guarantees.

It is reasonable to assume that all these functions would be performed under a federal regulatory system, although policies, procedures, and the use of resources might differ. A shift in emphasis to a prudential regulatory approach could result in significant changes in regulatory practices. The potential differences are discussed later in this chapter.

Providing insolvency guarantees is a policy decision that is not essential, but may be desirable, in a financial regulatory system. The states have established guaranty associations that cover the vast majority of failed insurers' obligations to individual policyholders.[7] Those guarantees enhance the security of policyholders and their confidence in insurers. However, they also diminish buyers' incentives to avoid high-risk insurers and, hence, can encourage greater risk-taking by insurers (Joskow 1973; Cummins 1988). That increases the public interest in effective solvency regulation to offset the moral hazard problem created by insolvency guarantees.[8]

Policing Market Practices. The states regulate various aspects of insurers' market practices and transactions, including prices, policy forms, marketing, underwriting, policy terminations, and claims handling. A strong argument can be made that regulatory ceilings on insurance prices are unnecessary and regulatory floors are impractical. Studies indicate that insurance markets are structurally competitive and that insurers do not possess sufficient market power to sustain excessive prices (Cummins and Weiss 1991; Klein 1999). In fact, many states have moved away from regulating insurance prices, and there is no clear evidence that consumers gain when states do regulate prices.[9] Indeed, price regulation can be very harmful when escalating costs and political considerations drive regulators to suppress rates (Harrington 1992).[10]

The arguments surrounding the regulation of other aspects of insurers' transactions are more complicated. The states tend to closely regulate the provisions of insurance contracts purchased by individual consumers and small businesses. The primary concern is that, without such regulation, some insurers might offer and some consumers might purchase policies containing major gaps in coverage. States also may utilize form regulation to ensure compliance with mandatory insurance requirements, legislatively mandated benefits, or the regulators' view of appropriate contract provisions. In that respect, form regulation may cross the line from necessary consumer protections to promoting social and political objectives.

Similarly, regulation of insurers' conduct in the areas of marketing, underwriting, policy terminations, and claims-handling may be beneficial in some respects and politically motivated in others. The states regulate market conduct primarily through periodic examinations of insurers' transactions and records, and through responses to consumer complaints. Some level of conduct monitoring, complaint resolution, and enforcement activity would be expected under any regulatory system. However, many believe that current state-market–conduct regulation is inefficient, and some conduct standards may exceed what is necessary for consumer protection.[11]

Other Insurance Regulatory Functions. The states perform a number of ancillary insurance regulatory functions, including:

- monitoring competition and market analysis;
- statistical reporting;
- residual market administration;
- providing consumer information;
- agent licensing and enforcement;

- antifraud enforcement;
- collection of premium taxes and other fees;
- legislative analysis and development of regulations.

While those activities are not as critical as financial and market regulation, they represent a small portion of regulatory budgets, and some may provide net benefits to consumers. Agent licensing and consumer services are the most significant of those activities and would likely be continued under any regulatory structure.

Regulatory Structures in Insurance and Banking

Every state and U.S. territory has a chief government official who is responsible for regulating insurance companies and markets. Most commissioners are appointed by the governor (or by a regulatory commission) for a set term or "at will," subject to legislative confirmation. Twelve states and one territory elect their insurance commissioners, who are more independent than appointed commissioners (NAIC 1997). However, even elected commissioners must still cooperate with other administration officials to achieve their objectives.

Current Role and Authority of Insurance Commissioners. Insurance commissioners are not autonomous, and they face a number of constraints in exercising their authority. Most important, regulators must act within the framework of insurance laws enacted by the legislature. Regulations promulgated by the commissioner are subject to review and approval by the legislature in some states. Regulatory actions are also subject to review and enforcement by the courts. In addition, resource constraints and the difficulties of supervising companies operating in multiple jurisdictions have caused states to defer primary solvency regulatory authority to the domiciliary commissioner (that is, the commissioner in the state where an insurer is domiciled or incorporated). Meanwhile, nondomiciliary regulators can exert considerable influence on nondomiciliary insurers through the regulators' ability to deny entry to their state's markets.[12]

Regulation of Insurers and Producers. All U.S. insurers are licensed in at least one state and are subject to solvency and market regulation in their state of domicile and in other states in which they are licensed to sell insurance. Reinsurers domiciled in the United States also are subject to the solvency regulation of their domiciliary state. Some U.S. and non-U.S. insurers write certain specialty and high-risk coverages on a nonadmitted or surplus-lines basis that are not subject to price and product regulation. States still control entry by surplus-lines carriers by imposing minimum solvency and trust requirements and by supervising surplus-lines brokers. Other alternative-market mechanisms, such as risk-retention groups and captives, are subject to some regulation in their state of domicile.

With the exception of solvency oversight by their domiciliary jurisdiction, reinsurers are not generally subject to direct financial and market regulation. Reinsurers are, however, regulated indirectly through the states' regulation of the primary insurers that are ceding business to reinsurers. Regulators control whether a ceding insurer can claim credit for reinsurance on its balance sheet, conditioned on whether the reinsurer meets certain financial or trust requirements imposed by regulators.

Insurance producers (that is, agents and brokers) also are subject to regulation. Producers must be licensed to sell insurance in a state and must comply with various laws and regulations governing their activities. State laws require most insurance transactions to be conducted by licensed producers. Regulators monitor producers' compliance with regulatory requirements and can rescind or suspend a producer's license, or can exact fines if the producer fails to comply.

Insurance is a large and important industry that continues to grow despite fierce competition from other financial institutions and alternative risk-management mechanisms. Tables 8–1 and 8–2 summarize key financial data on the property-liability and life-health insurance sectors. Together, U.S. property-liability and life-health insurers collect roughly $700 billion in premiums annually and control approximately $3 trillion in assets. There are somewhat fewer than 8,000 insurance companies domiciled in the United States, and their number has started to decline in recent years because of consolidation.

Role of the Federal Government. Tension between the federal government and the states over the regulation of insurance

TABLE 8–1
Property-Liability Insurance Trends, 1960–1995

	1960	1970	1980	1990	1995
Number of companies	n/a	2,800	2,953	3,899	3,358
Assets	30,132	55,315	197,678	556,314	765,230
Income	15,741	36,524	108,745	252,991	296,637
Net premiums written	95.1	94.3	89.6	86.9	87.6
Investment income	4.9	5.7	10.4	13.1	12.4
Market share of 10 largest insurers	34.4	36.8	38.2	40.3	40.0
Premiums/surplus	125.5	210.2	183.4	157.6	113.0
Return on net worth	n/a	11.6	13.1	8.5	9.0

n/a = not available.
SOURCE: National Association of Insurance Commissioners Financial Database, A. M. Best Aggregates and Averages Property-Casualty Edition, Oldwick, N.J.: Insurance Information Institute, Property/Casualty Insurance Fact Book, New York, N.Y. All various years.

TABLE 8–2
LIFE-HEALTH INSURANCE MARKET TRENDS, 1950–1995

	1950	1960	1970	1980	1990	1995
Number of companies	649	1,441	1,780	1,958	2,195	1,715
Assets ($millions)	64,020	119,576	207,254	479,210	1,408,208	2,143,500
% 10 largest companies	n/a	62.4	57.7	52.5	36.7	36.1
Income ($millions)	11,337	23,007	49,054	130,888	402,200	512,198
% Life insurance premiums	55.1	52.1	44.2	31.2	19.1	19.3
% Annuity considerations	8.3	5.8	7.6	17.1	32.1	31.2
% Health insurance premiums	8.8	17.5	23.2	22.4	14.5	15.7
% Investment income	18.3	18.7	20.7	25.9	27.8	27.4
% Other	9.5	5.8	4.4	3.3	6.5	6.4
Reserves ($millions)	54,946	98,473	167,779	390,339	1,196,967	1,812,325
% Life	n/a	71.9	68.8	50.7	29.1	28.2
% Annuities	n/a	27.2	29.1	46.5	68.1	68.3
% Health	n/a	0.9	2.1	2.8	2.8	3.5
Net rate of investment income (%)[a]	3.1	4.1	5.3	8.1	9.3	7.9
Capital ratio (%)[b]	n/a	n/a	9.7	9.2	8.5	10.7
Return on equity (%)	n/a	n/a	n/a	13.9	10.7	15.6

n/a = not available.
a. Net investment income divided by mean invested assets (including cash) less half of net investment income.
b. Capital plus surplus plus Asset Valuation Reserve (or Mandatory Securities Valuation Reserve prior to 1992 general account assets).
SOURCE: Klein 1995.

dates back to the mid-1800s (see Kimball and Heaney 1995).[13] That tension is created by the interstate operation of many insurers and their significant presence in the economy. On numerous occasions, the federal government has sought to exert greater control over the industry, and the states have fought back aggressively to hold on to their authority. The primacy of the states' authority over insurance was affirmed in numerous court decisions until the *South-Eastern Underwriters* case in 1944. In that case, the U.S. Supreme Court ruled that the commerce clause of the U.S. Constitution did apply to insurance and that the industry was subject to federal antitrust law. That decision prompted the states to support the enactment of the McCarran-Ferguson Act in 1945, which delegated regulation of insurance to the states, except in instances where federal law specifically supersedes state law.

The federal government affects state insurance regulatory policy and institutions in various ways. In several instances, Congress has instituted federal control over certain insurance markets or aspects of insurers' operations that were previously delegated to the states. In other cases, the federal government has established insurance programs, which are essentially exempt from state regulatory oversight—for example, flood and crop insurance. Even the threat of such interventions has spurred the states to take actions to forestall erosion of their regulatory authority.[14]

In a few instances, the federal government has set regulatory standards that the states are expected to enforce. In the case of Medicare supplement insurance, for example, Congress enacted loss ratio standards that the states were required to adopt to avoid relinquishing their oversight authority to the federal government. Additionally, Congress has significantly constrained state regulatory control over certain types of insurance entities, such as risk-retention groups and employer-funded health plans. That has made market regulation more difficult when bogus groups claim federal preemption to avoid state oversight. Finally, federal policies in a number of other areas, such as antitrust, international trade, law enforcement, taxation, and the regulation of banks and securities, have significant implications for the insurance industry and state regulation.

Role and Structure of the NAIC. Policing a large and diverse insurance industry that operates on an interstate basis is challenging for the individual states. Insurance commissioners have used their national association extensively in coordinating their regulatory activities. The NAIC is a private, nonprofit association of the chief insurance regulatory officials of the fifty states, the District of Columbia, and the four territories. It was established in 1871 to coordinate the supervision of multistate companies within a state regulatory framework, with special emphasis on insurers' financial condition. It expanded its activities to include market regulatory areas as those issues became more prominent. The NAIC functions both in an advisory capacity and as a service provider for state insurance departments.

The NAIC provides a vehicle by which the individual states can coordinate the exercise of their specific regulatory authorities. Commissioners use the NAIC to pool resources, discuss issues of common concern, and align their oversight of the industry. Collective action can enhance as well as constrain the power of individual states. The credence given to NAIC policy positions and its ability to organize its members are substantial levers that help to standardize insurance regulatory policy across the country, where the states deem standardization to be beneficial. At the same time, given its voluntary nature, the NAIC is relatively circumspect with regard to when and how it uses those levers. Ultimately, each state determines what actions it will take, as only the states have the regulatory authority to govern insurers and insurance markets.

The NAIC supports state regulatory efforts in a number of ways, including:

- maintaining extensive insurance databases and a computer network linking all insurance departments;
- developing and maintaining computer applications for regulators;
- analyzing and informing regulators as to the financial condition of insurance companies;
- coordinating examinations and regulatory actions with respect to troubled companies;
- establishing and certifying states' compliance with minimum financial regulation standards;

- providing financial, reinsurance, actuarial, legal, computer, and economic expertise to insurance departments;
- assigning credit-quality designations and valuing securities held by insurers;
- analyzing and listing nonadmitted alien insurers;
- developing uniform statutory financial statements and accounting rules for insurers;
- conducting education and training programs for insurance department staff;
- developing model laws and coordinating regulatory policy on significant insurance issues;
- conducting research and providing information on insurance and its regulation to state and federal officials and the general public.

State regulators are able to achieve considerable efficiencies by pooling resources through the centralized facilities provided by the NAIC. For example, it is much more efficient to have one central repository of insurer financial data than to have every department capture the same data from the same insurers. The objective is to allow states to focus their resources on the regulation of their markets and the solvency of their domiciliary companies, relying on support services from the NAIC. As of December 1998, the NAIC had a staff of 340 and an annual budget of approximately \$40 million. Almost half of NAIC revenues come from fees paid by insurers, with most of the remainder coming from the sale of database products, publications, and meeting registration fees. Insurance departments also pay member fees to the NAIC proportionate to the premiums written in their jurisdictions.

Current Banking Regulatory Structure

Banking in the United States is regulated by a mix of federal and state authorities, some with overlapping jurisdiction. Essentially, one or more federal agencies have at least some supervisory responsibilities for virtually all banking institutions. Banks can elect to be federally chartered or state chartered. Even state-chartered banks are subject to some oversight by the Federal Reserve or the Federal Deposit Insurance Corporation (FDIC), depending on their participation in those institutions. The Federal Reserve is the principal regulator of bank holding companies, the Office of the Comptroller of the Currency is the principal regulator of national banks, and the Office of Thrift Supervision regulates savings and loan associations. In addition, the National Credit Union Association (NCUA) regulates federally chartered credit unions. Finally, state regulators do have supervisory authority over state-chartered banks, but, as mentioned above, that authority is shared with the Federal Reserve Board if state banks choose to be members of the Federal Reserve System, or with the FDIC if they choose to be insured by the FDIC.

It is interesting to note in a general way the different philosophies of insurance and bank regulation. Both sets of regulators subject the institutions under their jurisdiction to solvency regulation audits, but they regulate market conduct issues differently. Insurance regulators scrutinize contract terms in individual policies, whole policies, prices of products, and even sales materials prior to a policy sale. That occurs when a policy or product is designed, as well as on a continuing basis.

Banking regulation as it relates to consumers and an institution's market conduct appears quite different. Regulators do not examine bank products to the same degree as insurance regulators, for example. There are numerous federal laws, such as the Truth in Lending Act, that specify how information is presented, but contracts are not reviewed or approved by an agency ex ante. Further, prices are not regulated. The general philosophy appears to be more of promoting or requiring disclosure rather than regulating the specifics of individual products.[15] That difference in philosophy can have important influences on the cost of regulation under a new structure of regulatory authority.

Optional Federal Chartering and Regulation of Insurers

Various options involving increased federal regulation of insurance have been discussed over the years, including optional federal chartering and regulation of insurance companies. In this chapter, we postulate one potential model of federal or state regulation of insurance for purposes of comparison. We assume that, under such a system, an insurance company could elect to be either federally chartered and regulated or state chartered and regulated. Federally regulated insurers would be authorized to sell insurance in any state without acquiring a state license or being subject to any state regulatory authority. A federal charter would preempt all state regulation regarding financial supervision or regulation relating to the status of an insurance company, as well as its market practices. That implies that the federal regulator would be responsible for supervising all aspects of such insurers, including solvency and market practices.

State-chartered insurers would be regulated much as they are under the current system. A state-chartered insurer would need to acquire a state license in every state in which it did business on an admitted basis. The domiciliary state would be the principal financial regulator. Nondomiciliary states would retain secondary financial regulatory responsibilities, as well as provide primary oversight of the market transactions of all state-chartered insurers (domestic and nondomestic) operating within their jurisdiction.

It is unclear how insolvency guarantees would be handled under such a system. The most logical approach would be to establish a federal guaranty association for federally regulated insurers and to retain the separate state guaranty associations for state-regulated insurers.[16] That would preclude the need for any federal oversight of state-chartered insurers. If state-chartered insurers participated in a federal guaranty association, however, then some degree of federal oversight would be needed to protect the federal government's interest in the insolvency guarantees provided to state insurers.[17]

The prospect for implementing regulatory reforms with the establishment of an optional federal regulatory system for insurers is an interesting one. It is possible, although not assured, that federal legislation could narrow the scope of the regulation of federally chartered insurers and also encourage the application of prudential solvency oversight concepts. Such policies could compel the states to reform their regulatory systems to avoid handicapping state-chartered insurers. But there is also the potential for "regulatory creep" at the federal level if interest groups were successful in pressuring federal officials to add regulations that serve their parochial objectives.

The sharing of authority and overlapping jurisdiction among regulatory agencies could worsen or improve the quality and efficiency of insurance regulation. For example, if the federal government were responsible for the solvency oversight of insurers but the states retained authority over their market practices, conflicts could arise. The states would have further incentives to suppress rates, which would undermine federal solvency objectives. Alternatively, federal and state authorities could be structured so as to create checks and balances and to discipline regulators. For example, if an insurer belonged to a federal insolvency guaranty system, the administrator of that system could be authorized to enforce solvency standards that would override politically motivated actions by other regulators that would increase the insurer's financial risk.

Regulatory Expenditures

The most obvious but smallest portion of insurance regulatory costs is direct expenditure on regulation. Since 1988, the NAIC has been conducting an annual survey of state insurance departments based on their budgets, staffing, and other aspects of their activities. The data from that survey provide a basis for assessing current expenditures on insurance regulation. The more difficult task is to determine how those costs might change under an alternative federal regulatory structure. The fact that state expenditures on insurance regulation represent a minor fraction of industry revenues suggests that even a large reduction in direct regulatory expenditures would have a small effect on total industry regulatory costs. At the same time, the number of regulatory personnel and their demands on insurers can also affect insurers' compliance costs.

Staffing and Budgets of State Insurance Departments. The size of state insurance departments varies significantly depending on the size of their markets and other factors. In 1997, the number of state insurance department personnel ranged from 24 in South Dakota and Wyoming to 1,135 in California (see table 8–3).[18] The insurance departments in the four U.S. territories have smaller staffs than the states. Total full-time equivalent staff for all departments combined amounted to 10,149, in addition to 1,700 contract staff. Insurance department staff includes actuaries, financial examiners and analysts, rates and forms

analysts, market conduct examiners, consumer service personnel, attorneys, fraud investigators, and systems analysts.

For fiscal year 1999, state insurance department budgets
ranged from $1.3 million in South Dakota to $127.5 million in
California, with a total combined budget for all departments of
approximately $797 million. The size of state insurance depart-
ments tends to vary with the volume of business that they regulate, although there is not a perfect correlation. States that have
more domiciliary companies, that regulate more intensively, or
that provide special services (for example, in-house liquidators)
tend to have larger staffs and budgets. Public and legislative support for insurance regulation also affects department resources.
The support services provided by the NAIC reduce the need for
expenditures by state insurance departments.

Insurance departments draw their funding, directly or indirectly, from: fees; assessments; and premium, retaliatory, and
other business and income taxes.[19] Those sources accounted for
98.7 percent of the $10 billion in revenues that states received
from the industry in 1997.[20] The relative "burden" of state insurance taxes and fees as a percentage of total premiums was 1.3
percent.[21] That figure has steadily declined since 1988, when it
was 1.7 percent.

Regulatory budgets represent only about 7.4 percent of revenues collected from insurers, but, presumably, those revenues
support other state services from which insurers (and their policyholders) benefit. That figure has increased steadily since 1986
(when the NAIC began to track it), when it was 4.5 percent. Some
insurance departments have partial or full dedicated funding
that allows them to fund their operations directly from fees and
assessments. Other insurance departments are funded solely
from general fund appropriations, which tend to impose greater
budget constraints, as those departments are forced to compete
directly with other state agencies for scarce resources.

The states have significantly increased the resources devoted to insurance regulation in recent years. From fiscal year
1990 to fiscal year 1999, funding for state insurance departments
increased by 80 percent (see figure 8–1). The increased funding
has been used primarily to raise staffing levels, boost salaries to
attract and retain more qualified staff, and improve automation
to enhance staff productivity. Departments have significantly

TABLE 8–3
INSURANCE DEPARTMENT RESOURCES IN 1997

State	Number of Insurers Domestic	Licensed nondomestic	Direct Premiums Written	Revenues	FY 1999 Budget	FTE Staff
Alabama	89	1,380	$13,330,640,868	$160,700,014	$9,873,951	69.0
Alaska	10	1,088	1,572,340,407	33,483,294	4,192,400	50.0
American Samoa	N/A	N/A	2,517,242	N/A	N/A	N/A
Arizona	517	1,548	12,349,206,000	159,693,487	5,404,700	138.0
Arkansas	83	1,443	4,970,791,241	114,925,247	6,037,439	102.0
California	245	1,279	72,977,550,532	1,345,971,425	127,467,000	1,134.8
Colorado	90	1,372	13,114,189,038	117,229,739	7,900,000	95.4
Connecticut	135	1,000	13,976,729,766	222,671,522	15,564,918	164.0
Delaware	145	1,250	3,108,518,515	57,844,500	4,723,900	67.0
District of Columbia	15	1,301	3,679,096,915	47,216,450	7,000,067	62.0
Florida	477	1,858	33,292,936,170	465,904,567	64,104,297	1,043.0
Georgia	112	1,484	18,676,739,133	444,725,115	17,241,858	168.0
Guam	5	90	219,718,617	N/A	1,337,730	8.0
Hawaii	86	888	4,540,992,000	80,064,656	5,513,038	47.0
Idaho	28	1,476	2,544,685,948	52,876,200	5,101,400	64.5
Illinois	503	1,467	41,246,624,335	208,898,251	25,704,900	353.0
Indiana	204	1,666	16,289,715,880	141,171,092	4,673,237	84.0
Iowa	228	1,386	7,078,414,176	121,352,272	6,780,647	90.0
Kansas	57	1,497	5,810,540,435	140,115,654	8,004,227	154.5
Kentucky	72	1,457	8,741,582,715	155,689,965	14,051,000	174.0
Louisiana	170	1,498	10,828,176,796	189,238,852	28,227,660	261.0
Maine	32	867	3,654,010,631	47,022,101	6,074,579	72.0
Maryland	106	1,374	11,949,994,966	182,476,085	15,379,409	249.0
Massachusetts	105	1,163	27,585,573,109	26,741,423	8,422,834	163.0
Michigan	152	1,245	33,934,211,000	184,061,182	16,398,500	127.0
Minnesota	210	1,231	15,332,392,246	169,979,326	7,024,299	121.0

Mississippi	77	1,446	4,471,202,770	113,922,784	6,395,409	114.0
Missouri	309	1,529	15,065,924,689	186,132,914	12,185,653	210.0
Montana	28	1,408	1,675,033,324	37,601,561	2,094,337	43.0
Nebraska	129	1,453	4,607,803,553	54,171,918	5,929,949	92.8
Nevada	36	1,434	4,168,605,397	103,927,948	4,189,275	65.0
New Hampshire	53	800	2,757,743,796	59,897,326	3,423,418	51.0
New Jersey	112	1,085	25,136,769,913	321,293,000	33,598,000	402.0
New Mexico	22	1,521	3,232,124,928	85,157,043	3,755,800	77.0
New York	395	723	68,719,274,707	921,734,925	96,827,000	865.0
North Carolina	111	1,207	20,136,932,922	288,027,916	33,088,000	388.0
North Dakota	55	1,380	1,878,393,939	27,465,475	2,917,657	45.5
Ohio	310	1,452	30,610,882,420	384,341,389	22,122,025	248.0
Oklahoma	123	1,470	6,228,947,887	138,785,717	6,843,245	122.0
Oregon	116	1,498	8,192,702,017	89,806,213	6,389,145	98.5
Pennsylvania	350	1,318	46,203,910,291	224,105,000	19,039,000	274.0
Puerto Rico	N/A	N/A	1,685,529,391	N/A	N/A	N/A
Rhode Island	35	1,017	3,691,816,758	47,284,787	3,365,084	53.0
South Carolina	53	1,424	7,405,544,356	103,867,326	6,179,489	107.0
South Dakota	60	1,444	2,003,604,572	39,441,485	1,295,371	24.0
Tennessee	130	1,534	15,834,515,190	278,049,932	5,981,400	91.0
Texas	572	1,529	52,472,811,479	770,488,033	48,330,067	1,003.2
U.S. Virgin Islands	N/A	N/A	52,769,496	N/A	N/A	21.0
Utah	54	1,485	5,113,902,303	74,095,962	4,130,900	71.5
Vermont	329	778	1,962,380,659	31,883,710	4,407,168	49.0
Virginia	88	1,330	17,824,345,743	249,922,301	16,855,018	190.0
Washington	80	1,303	14,469,167,006	229,582,817	11,633,976	164.0
West Virginia	22	1,230	3,466,298,720	105,091,895	4,560,823	72.0
Wisconsin	342	1,476	15,600,165,174	104,186,783	7,917,200	121.7
Wyoming	5	1,211	1,026,964,622	12,100,537	1,303,843	24.0
Total	7,872		$766,503,956,703	$9,952,419,116	$796,962,242	10,148.5
Mean	151	1,304	$13,936,435,576	$195,145,473	$15,326,197	191

N/A = not available. FTE = full-time equivalent.
SOURCE: *Insurance Department Resources Report 1977* (NAIC).

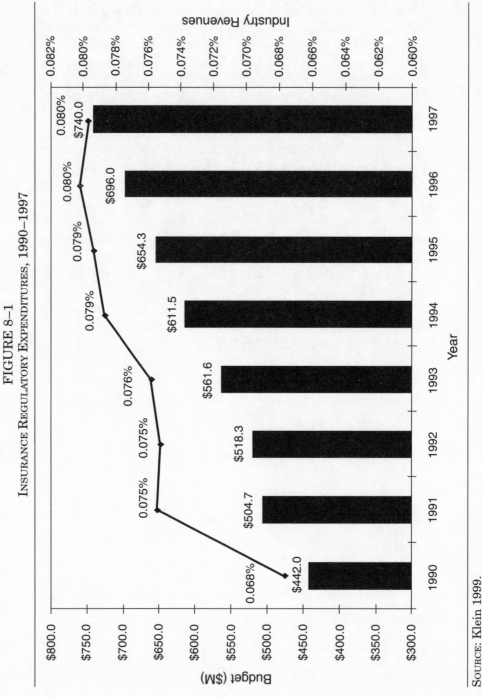

FIGURE 8–1
INSURANCE REGULATORY EXPENDITURES, 1990–1997

SOURCE: Klein 1999.

enhanced their use of computers and upgraded their information systems. The increase in staff and enhanced automation has allowed regulators to substantially boost the quality and intensity of their financial oversight of insurers, as well as expand consumer protection activities. Staff and budget growth in many departments have begun to plateau as they meet their resource objectives.

Figure 8–1 also shows total regulatory expenditures as a percentage of industry premiums and investment income. We can see from that figure that regulatory expenditures have increased, but have remained a very small fraction of industry revenues (roughly 0.08 percent), over the past decade. With budgets leveling out and no new major state initiatives planned, relative regulatory expenditures are unlikely to increase in the near future unless the states were given additional responsibilities or compelled to further enhance the quality or intensity of their oversight activities.

While the NAIC data do not indicate how regulatory expenditures are divided among the various regulatory functions, that division might be inferred from the breakdown of personnel by job category. Table 8–4 shows the allocation of regulatory staff (including contract employees) by position and function. Regulators working in the financial area represent 21.9 percent of total

TABLE 8–4
ALLOCATION OF REGULATORY STAFF BY FUNCTION, 1997

Position	Number	Percentage
Financial examiners	1,198	10.1
Financial analysts	400	3.4
Liquidators	927	7.8
Company licensing	66	0.6
Rate/Form analysts	676	5.7
Market conduct examiners	425	3.6
Actuaries	293	2.5
Consumer services	1,462	12.3
Producer licensing	381	3.2
Other	6,020	50.8
Total staff	11,848	100.0

NOTE: Figures include department and contract employees.
SOURCE: *Insurance Department Resources Report 1997* (NAIC).

staff. Rates and forms analysts constitute 5.7 percent, market conduct examiners 3.6 percent, and consumer services staff 12.3 percent of total staff. If we assume that the allocation of regulatory expenditures and supervisory and support personnel follows the allocation of line personnel, financial regulation would account for close to 50 percent of total expenditures. That allocation may be significant in terms of the effect of reconfiguring state regulatory priorities or changing the institutional structure for regulation, as discussed below.

Implications of Changes in Regulatory Activities or Structures. It is conceivable that the states could reduce the number of regulatory personnel and associated expenditures by limiting their market regulatory functions to the most essential areas. Eliminating prior approval requirements for rates and forms in all lines and curtailing filing requirements for most commercial products could reduce the need for rates and forms analysts and actuaries. Indeed, many states are already moving in that direction. According to our estimates in table 8–5, a 75-percent reduction in rates and forms personnel would reduce regulatory expenditures by $75 million, or 10 percent. There would still be a need for some personnel and expenditures in that area, for monitoring and enforcement activities. Further, those changes would be unlikely to reduce the number of market conduct examiners and consumer service personnel.

It is not clear that significant reductions in financial regulatory personnel would be possible under the current state system without impairing the quality of financial oversight. Although a prudential regulatory approach might be more effective and efficient than the current prescriptive regulatory approach, it is not obvious that the latter would require fewer personnel and reduce associated expenditures.

Moving to an optional federal regulatory system could reduce expenditures in some areas, depending on the functions that were performed. Table 8–6 compares the regulatory expenditures of state insurance departments (including the NAIC) with other financial regulators. That comparison suggests that state insurance regulation is relatively costly, although some of that disparity could be caused by differences in the scope of regulatory activities as well as the regulatory jurisdictional overlap among the various agencies. In relation to the amount of assets of regulated entities, insurance regulatory expenditures are the highest at .023 percent; that percentage ranges from .011 percent to .019 percent for other financial regulatory agencies.[22]

Grace and Phillips (1999) estimate some parameters on the costs of regulating the insurance industry at the state level by examining the multiproduct cost efficiency of the state-based regulatory system. They find that the largest one-third of the states experience decreasing returns to scale in the production of regulation. The smaller states, in contrast, experience increasing returns to scale. Grace and Phillips assert that the reason the largest states experience decreasing returns to scale is because of a free-rider problem that exists between the larger and smaller states in terms of solvency regulation. If the federal government took over the solvency regulatory function, then the free-rider problem could be eliminated. Regulatory expenditures also would be reduced to the extent that state insurance departments have to duplicate some of the fixed investments in infrastructure that support solvency regulation. Grace and Phillips also find little evidence of economies of scope in state regulatory functions. Thus, a separation between federal and state regulation on a functional basis would not necessarily increase total regulatory expenditures.

Given that the states rely primarily on insurers' domiciliary states for solvency oversight, moving to a federal system would not necessarily significantly reduce the number of personnel in that area, although the need for personnel to perform secondary monitoring of nondomiciliary insurers would be eliminated. As noted above, there also might be some savings with respect to maintaining a technological infrastructure for financial regulation by housing that responsibility under one organization. The savings would be lower if a significant number of insurers remained chartered and regulated at the state level. For the sake of discussion, a 25-percent reduction in financial regulatory personnel under a federal system would imply annual savings of $100 million, representing 13 percent of total regulatory expenditures.

If the current level of market regulation were performed by a federal agency based on a uniform set of regulations, there could be a significant reduction in the number of rates-and-forms

TABLE 8-5

Tobit Regression Results: Measurement of Costs Implications of Multistate Licensing and "Restrictive" Regulation of Property-Liability Industry, 1997

Variable	Variable Description	Ratio of Total Expenses to Premiums	Ratio of Salary Expenses to Premiums	Ratio of Claims Expenses to Premiums	Ratio of Licenses and Fees to Premiums
One	Intercept	6.6325[a]	6.4564[a]	2.6196[a]	0.4224[a]
		(0.8296)	(0.8290)	(0.4138)	(0.0893)
DIR	Direct marketing dummy	-0.0175	-0.0165	0.0148	-0.0048[c]
		(0.0251)	(0.0252)	(0.0128)	(0.0028)
Stock	Stock company dummy	-0.0065	-0.0075	0.0088	-0.0028
		(0.0251)	(0.0252)	(0.0128)	(0.0028)
LTOTLIC	Log of total licenses	0.0498[a]	0.0037[a]	0.0107[a]	0.0001[b]
		(0.0074)	(0.0006)	(0.0038)	(0.0001)
RES	Log of premiums written in restrictive environments	-0.0008	-0.0023	0.0006	-0.0002
		(0.0019)	(0.0020)	(0.0010)	(0.0002)
LGROUP	Log of group premiums	0.0075	0.0063	0.0089[a]	0.0020[a]
		(0.0059)	(0.0059)	(0.0030)	(0.0006)

		(1)	(2)	(3)	(4)
LAUTO	Log of total auto premiums	0.0041[b]	0.0049[a]	0.0006	0.0002
		(0.0017)	(0.0017)	(0.0009)	(0.0002)
LHOME	Log of total home owners premiums	0.0023	0.0028	−0.0021[b]	−0.0003
		(0.0018)	(0.0018)	(0.0009)	(0.0002)
LCOMP	Log of commercial property premiums (allied lines + fire)	0.0017	0.0017	0.0028[a]	−0.0004[b]
		(0.0017)	(0.0017)	(0.0009)	(0.0002)
LCOMPR	Log of commercial premiums (farmers and commercial multiperil)	0.0044[b]	0.0044[b]	0.0019[c]	0.0004[c]
		(0.0021)	(0.0021)	(0.0011)	(0.0002)
Size	Log of total premiums	−0.6567[a]	−0.6300[a]	−0.2716[a]	−0.0469[a]
		(0.0927)	(0.0926)	(0.0463)	(0.0100)
Size²	Log of total premiums²	0.0159[a]	0.0151[a]	0.0064[a]	0.0012[a]
		(0.0026)	(0.0026)	(0.0013)	(0.0003)
Psuedo R²		undefined	0.0458	0.028634	0.0148
OLS R²		0.18	0.21	0.16	0.06
	Elasticity between total licenses and expense ratios	0.1	0.14	0.08	0.03

NOTE: Regression weighted by the log of total assets. Standard errors are in parentheses.
a. Significant at the 0.01 level, b. at 0.05 level, c. at 0.1 level.
SOURCE: Author.

TABLE 8–6
FINANCIAL INSTITUTION REGULATORY COSTS, 1997

Regulatory Body	No. of Reg. Entities	Budget $Millions	Asset $Billions	Percent Budget/Assets	$, Per Entity Cost
State insurance department and NAIC[a]	7,872	785.4	3,433	0.023	99,767
Federal Reserve System[b]	8,007	517.0	4,791	0.011	64,569
Office of Comptroller of the Currency	2,597	350.0	2,894	0.012	134,771
FDIC[c]	10,922	605.0	5,607	0.011	55,393
Office of Thrift Supervision	1,215	151.0	777	0.019	124,280
National Credit Union Association	11,238	46.3	351	0.013	4,120

NOTE: The Federal Reserve Board has overlapping jurisdiction with the Office of Thrift Supervision and the Office of the Comptroller of the Currency.
a. Includes property-liability and life, health and annuity companies.
b. Includes the number of state member banks and the number of separate banks belonging to bank holding companies.
c. FDIC has financial regulatory authority over insured banks.
SOURCE: Official budget documents or annual reports for the various agencies.

regulatory personnel and expenditures. That is because under the current system, each state regulates the market activities of all insurers operating within its jurisdiction, and there is little if any reliance on an insurer's domiciliary state for that regulation. At the same time, the decrease in personnel performing market conduct examinations and responding to consumer inquiries and complaints might be small. If we assume that moving to federal regulation would reduce the need for market regulatory personnel by 25 percent, the implied savings would be $100 million annually, or 13 percent of total expenditures.

The discussion above suggests that federal regulation of both insurer solvency and market activities could reduce direct regulatory expenditures by as much as $200 million annually, or 25 percent. That kind of reduction would bring relative insurance regulatory expenditures closer to those for other financial institutions. However, that figure represents only .002 percent of industry revenues, so its total effect on industry costs would be minimal. Moreover, if a significant number of insurers remained under state regulation, the savings would be lower. Much more important are the expenditures that insurers must make to comply with state regulations. The next subsection discusses these costs in a qualitative sense. Toward the end of the chapter we develop empirical quantitative estimates of those costs.

Direct Compliance Costs

Complying with state regulations requires insurers to perform a number of tasks with associated expenditures on personnel and other expenses. Those tasks include:

- submitting applications for licensing;
- submitting financial and statistical reports;
- paying for independent audits and regulatory examinations;
- preparing and submitting rates and forms filings;
- ensuring internal compliance with state regulations;
- responding to regulatory inquiries;
- paying taxes, fees, and assessments.

There is little doubt that a state-based regulatory system significantly increases insurers' regulatory compliance costs. Many of the activities listed above must be performed for every state in which a company conducts business on a licensed basis. The additional compliance costs imposed by state financial regulation are probably less significant than the additional compliance costs imposed by state market regulation. The states have generally adopted uniform NAIC financial reporting forms, although some states require special adjustments for supplemental reports. Also, the states generally rely on financial examinations performed by an insurer's domiciliary state or NAIC-coordinated zone exams. It is rare for a nondomiciliary state to conduct its own separate financial examination.

Filing separate licensing applications in each state is probably the greatest concern of insurers in the financial regulatory area. The average market value of a state license has been estimated at $50,000, which provides some indication of the cost of the licensing process. In response to industry concerns about repetitive and inefficient state licensing processes, a number of states and the NAIC are working on an approach that would significantly reduce the duplication of effort in filing for multiple state licenses (Klein 1999).

It is apparent that the costs of complying with individual state market regulations are high. The states' market regulations and procedures vary much more than their financial regulations and procedures. An insurer must make a separate rate and form filing for each product it sells, in every state in which it sells the product. Any change in rates or policy forms also must be filed and justified. Moreover, the regulations and procedural requirements governing those products and filings differ by state. Extensive filings are required and often go through a lengthy process and frequent iterations before they are approved. An insurer also may have to undergo regulatory hearings on some filings. A significant number of insurer personnel are dedicated to the preparation and process of state rate and form filings.

Insurers also complain that complying with state market conduct regulations is costly. Unlike financial examinations, many states perform separate market conduct examinations on domiciliary as well as nondomiciliary companies. Consequently, a company may undergo a number of market conduct examinations every year. The concept of single or coordinated market conduct examinations has been rejected by state regulators on the basis that state laws and regulations governing market conduct vary significantly among states. Variation in state market conduct standards further increases insurer compliance costs.

Implications of Changes in Regulatory Activities or Structure. Some savings in compliance costs associated with financial regulation probably could be achieved by moving to a federal regulatory system. Insurers under a federal charter would need to prepare reports for and respond to inquiries from only one regulator, rather than multiple regulators. However, given the current degree of uniformity among states and reliance on the domiciliary regulator, it is unlikely that federal regulation per se would result in huge relative reductions in financial compliance costs. Movement to a prudential financial regulatory approach could further reduce some of the paperwork and internal compliance that monitoring imposes on insurers.

Relatively larger savings in compliance costs could be achieved by reducing the scope of market regulation or imposing greater uniformity through a federal system. Complying with a uniform set of market regulations and filing with only one regulatory agency would greatly reduce insurers' need for compliance personnel and other expenditures. Confining market regulation to key areas such as policy forms for individual consumer products, marketing practices, and claims-handling would further lower compliance costs. Some sense of the potential magnitude of such savings is provided below, where we estimate current compliance costs.

Effects of Regulation on Market Efficiency

Finally, we come to the most obscure but potentially most significant area of regulatory costs—the implicit or intangible effects of regulation on market efficiency. By that we mean the effect of regulation on social welfare or combined consumer and producer surplus, beyond the tangible expenditures on regulation and regulatory compliance. Regulation has the potential both to increase and to decrease consumer and producer surplus. When regulation corrects significant market failures, it potentially increases social welfare. For example, if regulation reduces insolvency costs and increases consumer confidence, and if those "benefits" exceed other costs imposed by such regulation, then there should be a net addition to social welfare. Conversely, when regulation restricts consumer choice and distorts market decisions and there is no commensurate benefit to consumers, then social welfare is reduced. Below we discuss how those intangible benefits and costs might be affected by changes in regulatory policies and structures.

Insolvency Costs. There are some data on insurance insolvency costs. Since state guaranty associations were established in the late 1960s, national organizations have tracked the amount of payments made to policyholders of insolvent insurers and assessed back against all the members of the guaranty associations. Figures 8–2 and 8–3 chart the number of insurer insolvencies and guaranty association assessments. Total payments and assessments amount to $10.3 billion over the years 1976–1995. On an annual basis, guaranty association assessments have averaged less than 0.5 percent of industry premiums. Those figures do not include insolvency costs that were not covered by guaranty associations, although those costs are probably relatively small. Also, the intangible costs of solvency regulation on market transactions are not reflected in those figures.

Assessments rose sharply in the middle 1980s for property-liability insurers because of an increase in the frequency and size of insurer failures. A similar pattern occurred slightly later for life-health insurers. The increase in insurer insolvencies can be attributed largely to external economic shocks, but there were also criticisms of the quality of state insurance regulation (see U.S. Congress [Dingell Report] 1990; U.S. General Accounting Office 1991). Since the early 1990s, insolvencies and insolvency costs have fallen dramatically and have remained at a low level.

The burden of insurer insolvency costs is distributed among policyholders, taxpayers, and the owners of insurance companies (Barrese and Nelson 1994). Insurers can pass a significant portion of guaranty association assessments on to policyholders through rate surcharges, and on to taxpayers through state and federal tax credits and deductions.[23]

It is possible that federal regulation could reduce insurer insolvency costs, but the savings could be small given that insolvency costs have been relatively low in recent years. Federal

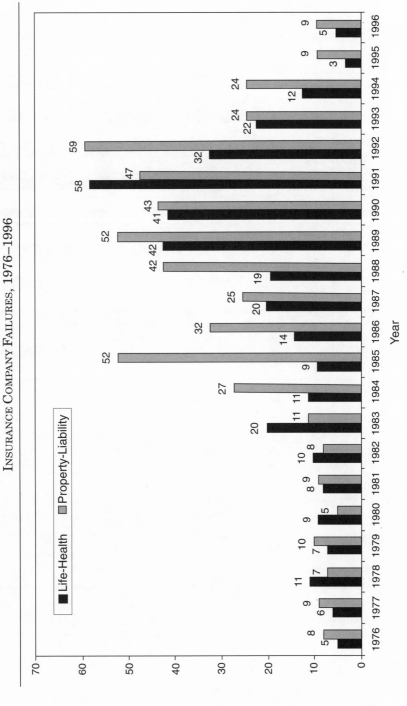

FIGURE 8–2

INSURANCE COMPANY FAILURES, 1976–1996

Life-Health   Property-Liability

SOURCE: A. M. Best and National Association of Insurance Commissioners.

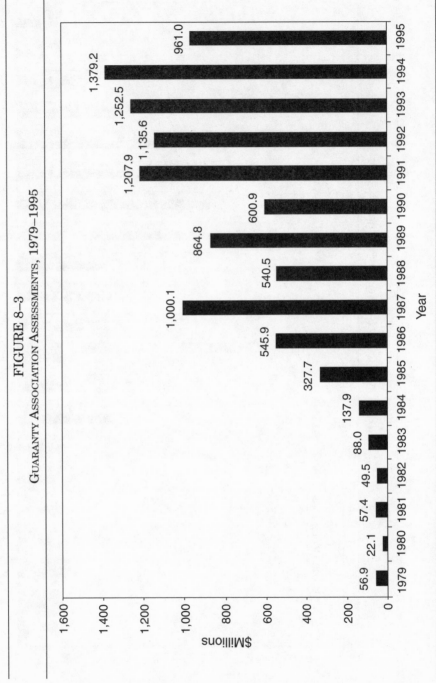

FIGURE 8–3

Guaranty Association Assessments, 1979–1995

Source: National Conference of Insurance Guaranty Funds and National Organization of Life-Health Guaranty Associates.

solvency regulation of interstate insurers could be more effective and efficient, however. Also, state receiverships of insolvent insurers have been criticized for their inefficiency and high expenses. Bohn and Hall (1998) found that the cost of insurance company insolvencies was three times as high as bank insolvencies when insolvency costs were measured in relation to pre-insolvency assets. The impact of federal solvency regulation would depend heavily on how federal regulators were to respond to and counter new economic pressures on insurers, or on other factors that would prompt insurers to greatly increase their financial risk. In other words, if insurers were threatened by a major solvency crisis, federal regulators might be in a better position to use the power and resources of the federal government to ameliorate the crisis.

But some have expressed the concern that a singular regulator can also be a problem if that regulator implements bad policies. Supporters of state insurance regulation point to the failures of federal thrift and bank regulators in the 1980s. One advantage of the current state system of regulation is that non-domiciliary states provide a check on omissions by an insurer's domiciliary regulator.

Other Market Corrections and Distortions. In addition to affecting insolvency costs, insurance regulation potentially imposes other market corrections and distortions. Financial regulation imposes some market costs even if it is deemed to provide net benefits to policyholders. Financial regulation raises barriers to entry, restricts insurers' risk and investment portfolios, and limits the products and terms they can offer. Those costs are probably affected more by the states' approach to financial regulation than by the institutional structure for regulation. Moving to a prudential regulatory approach could substantially reduce the market costs of arbitrary legal restrictions on insurers' investments and other transactions. Simply shifting the enforcement of prescriptive regulations from the states to a federal regulator would seem to have little effect on intangible regulatory costs.

The intangible costs of the current system of market regulation are probably much greater. Price regulation distorts market signals and incentives for efficient risk management. For example, if rates are suppressed, insurance buyers have less incentive to lower risk and control losses. Restrictions on policy forms limit consumers' options and ability to purchase contracts that might better fit their needs and preferences. Some market conduct regulations also may distort insurance transactions.[24] Moreover, the delays involved in filing and getting rates and forms approved impose additional market costs.

As with financial regulation, the optimality of market regulation has to be judged in terms of both benefits and costs. Benefits to consumers are more likely to exceed market costs for the most essential market regulatory functions identified earlier in this chapter. Market costs likely exceed consumer benefits for nonessential functions, such as price regulation and prior approval requirements for commercial insurance contracts.

There are differing views on whether assigning market regulation to the states benefits consumers. On the one hand, the necessity of dealing with multiple regulators and varying state requirements imposes some additional intangible costs on insurance transactions. For example, the need to make filings in multiple states could add to the delays in introducing rate and product changes.

On the other hand, economic theory suggests that the Pareto optimal provision of a public good such as regulation will be achieved when it is produced by the most decentralized layer of government capable of internalizing all the economic costs and benefits associated with regulation (Inman and Rubinfeld 1997; Oates 1972). The primary advantage of having more localized units of government produce public goods is that smaller jurisdictions are more likely to be responsive to the tastes and preferences of the local citizens and therefore can tailor the quality and level of output to maximize their welfare. That advantage, however, must be weighed against the inefficiencies of decentralization that could include possible spillover effects between jurisdictions and the possibility that the jurisdiction may be too small to capture any economies of scale that may be associated with the production of the regulation.

Supporters of state regulation argue that it is more responsive to the needs and preferences of consumers in a state. The strength of that argument partly depends on how much the regulatory needs and preferences of consumers vary among states. It is not obvious that the citizens of New Jersey have significantly different preferences for insurer regulatory policies than the citizens of Illinois have. The greatest advantage of state regulation may not be the ability to vary regulatory policies, but rather the responsiveness of regulatory personnel in addressing complaints and providing other consumer services.

Estimation of Regulatory Compliance Costs

Regulators can impose costs on society that are like the deadweight losses imposed by taxation. Regulation that increases the cost of doing business without an associated benefit is thus borne by capital owners, employees, and consumers, and it is not necessarily clear which group bears the incidence of this type of regulation. Regardless of who bears the burden, regulation can raise the cost of a product, decrease returns to equity owners, or lower the employee's wages.

There are potentially many ways to show the cost of regulation imposed on the industry. We choose a simple way that looks at both the property-liability industry and the life and health insurance industry. We focus on the compliance costs measured by those increased costs associated with doing business in "restrictive regulatory climates" or, alternatively, in each additional state where the insurer decides to do business.

Data and Methodology. If regulation imposes costs on a firm, then it may show up in the expenses of the firm. Higher expenses, all other things held constant, should exist in those firms that are more heavily regulated. We employ four measures of expenses for the property-liability industry and three measures for the life and health industry, which are obtained from the NAIC Annual Statement Tapes at Georgia State University. The first (E_PRAT) is the ratio of total expenses to total direct premiums written.[25] That shows the effect of regulation on the total expenses (relative to premiums) of the firm. The other ratios reflect salary expenses to total premiums written (S_PRAT), claims adjustment expenses to total premiums written (C_PRAT), and licenses and fees to total premiums (F_PRAT). Changes in S_PRAT are presumed to reflect the additional employee time spent in dealing with regulation and can be thought of as an indication of compliance costs. F_PRAT represents the (nontax) costs paid to the state for regulatory services. Changes in F_PRAT reflect the additional costs of license fees. Finally, for the property-liability industry we also estimate C_PRAT to reflect the cost of resolving claims. Changes in C_PRAT can be thought of as the effect of regulation on resolving claims.

Table 8–7, panel A, shows the property-liability industry's descriptive statistics. We see that E_PRAT has a mean of approximately 40 percent, while S_PRAT is approximately 11 percent. C_PRAT is approximately 8.5 percent, and F_PRAT is less than one-half of 1 percent. Panel B describes similar statistics for the life and health industry. E_PRAT is approximately 24 percent, while S_PRAT is approximately 9 percent. Finally, F_PRAT is about one half of 1 percent. We employ each of those ratios as a way of measuring, in a gross sense, the effect of complying with regulatory policies on the firm's costs.[26]

Conning and Co. (1997) undertakes a semi-objective analysis of states based on its regulatory environment.[27] It examines the types of law governing the insurance industry. Those include the type of rating law used for personal lines, the status of various tort reform measures, whether the commissioner is appointed or elected, and the amount of regulatory personnel in the state. Conning and Co. also employs some undisclosed qualitative assessments to obtain a ranking of states based on the states' regulatory environment. Conning and Co. identified the bottom ten states in its report, and we refer to those states as having restrictive regulatory environments. That determination reflects Conning and Co.'s assessment that the state has a restrictive regulatory environment in the personal lines business.[28] For the property-liability industry we estimate the total number of premiums written in each state with a restrictive environment for auto and homeowners insurance. For the life industry we sum the premiums written in life, accident and health, and annuities. The log of the premiums written in restrictive environments (RES) is employed to determine the effect of nonessential regulation on the cost to the firm. Extraneous or nonessential regulation might include that type of regulation not consistent with the essential insurance regulation described earlier in this chapter.

In this simple analysis, we employ additional control variables. Because of differences in the life and health markets and property-liability markets, the estimated regressions are not exactly parallel but were estimated to be similar, so that basic comparisons could be made. The first control variable is a dummy variable used to determine whether the company is a stock company (STOCK). The second (DIR) is a dummy variable that controls for whether the insurer primarily employs a direct (rather than agency) marketing system. The third control variable is related to membership in a group. A group structure can conceivably provide services across the group less expensively than individual companies can. Thus, there may be group economies of scope. We measure that variable as the log of premiums written by the group (LGROUP). The fourth is a size variable that is the log of the total direct premiums (and annuity considerations) written. That is employed along with its square as an attempt to control for potential economies of scale of the firm.[29]

For each industry we also add some control variables to reflect the business mix of the company. For the property-liability industry we log the sum of the premiums written in auto (LAUTO), commercial property (including allied lines and fire) (LCOMPR), commercial multiperil (including farm owner's multiperil) (LCOMP), and homeowner's multiperil (LHOME). For the life industry we log the sum of life premiums (LLIFE) and accident and health premiums (LAH).

Empirical Results. Table 8–5 shows our results for the property-liability industry, while table 8–8 provides the results for the life and health industry. We estimate a tobit model for both industries, as the expense ratios are bounded by 0 and 1. To account for significant heteroskedasticity we estimated a weighted model where the weight is the log of total assets. In terms of organizational form for the property-liability industry, stock companies do not appear to have significantly higher fee expense ratios, and no significant relationship was found for any other expense ratio. For the life industry, stocks had significantly lower expense ratios for total expenses and salary expenses.[30] For the direct agency system variable, life expense ratios appeared lower, but there was not a similar pattern in the property-liability insurance industry.[31]

The effect of size is also significant in almost every model. For total expenses, salaries, claims costs, and fees, the data

TABLE 8–7
DESCRIPTIVE STATISTICS

Panel A: Property-Liability Industry

Variable	Variable Description	Mean	Std. Dev.	Minimum	Maximum
STOCK	Stock company dummy	0.784764	0.411235	0	1
RES	Log of premiums written in restrictive environments	3.57609	5.93818	0.693147	21.6868
DIR	Direct marketing dummy	0.182588	0.386562	0	1
LTOTLIC	Log of total licenses	2.39186	1.49546	0	3.98898
LAUTO	Log of total auto premiums	12.8304	6.77185	0	23.4118
LHOME	Log of total home owners premiums	9.5	7.4914	0	22.4703
LCOMPR	Log of commercial premiums (farmers and commercial multiperil)	10.0981	6.5081	0	19.6574
LCOMP	Log of commercial property premiums (allied lines + fire)	10.1095	7.4453	0	20.7296
LGROUP	Log of group premiums	19.5393	2.2208	13.9798	24.2529
SIZE	Log of total premiums	17.8227	1.6491	13.9033	23.8877
E_PRAT	Total expenses/Total DPW	0.4020	0.2641	0.0023	1
S_PRAT	Salary expenses/Total DPW	0.0853	0.1386	0	1
C_PRAT	Claims expenses/Total DPW	0.1091	0.1425	0	1
F_PRAT	Licenses and fees/Total DPW	0.0039	0.0277	0	0.7464

n = 827

Panel B: Life and Health Industry

Variable	Variable Description	Mean	Std. Dev.	Minimum	Maximum
STOCK	Stock company dummy	0.9092	0.2875	0	1
DIR	Direct marketing dummy	0.0719	0.2584	0	1
LTOTL	Log of total licenses	0.3701	0.3459	0	0.6931
LLIFE	Log of total U.S. life premiums	15.6956	2.7340	3.8067	23.0427
LAH	Log of total A & H premiums	10.7578	7.5964	0	22.5730
RES	Log of premiums written in restrictive environments	10.3113	7.7174	0	21.9391
LGROUP	Log of group premiums	16.9715	2.5017	11.6239	23.4507
SIZE	Log of total premiums and annuity considerations	16.8864	2.4173	11.6239	23.4089
E_PRAT	Total expenses/Total premiums and annuity considerations	0.2634	0.1916	0.0017	0.9764
S_PRAT	Salary expenses/Total premiums and annuity considerations	0.0908	0.0878	0	0.5785
F_PRAT	Licenses and fees/Total premiums and annuity considerations	0.0061	0.0115	0	0.1794

n = 1,001
SOURCE: Author.

TABLE 8–8

Tobit Regression Results: Measurement of Costs Implications of Multistate Licensing and "Restrictive" Regulation Life and Health Industry

Variable	Variable Description	Ratio of Total Expenses to Premiums	Ratio of Salary Expenses to Premiums	Ratio of Fees to Premiums
One	Intercept	1.8433[a]	0.3908[a]	0.1519[a]
		(0.2223)	(0.1205)	(0.0130)
Dir	Direct marketing dummy	−0.0359[c]	−0.0191[c]	0.0015
		(0.0197)	(0.0105)	(0.0012)
Stock	Stock company dummy	−0.0404[b]	−0.0205[b]	0.0010
		(0.0177)	(0.0094)	(0.0010)
LTOTL	Log of total licenses	0.0574[a]	0.0252[b]	0.0077[a]
		(0.0217)	(0.0116)	(0.0013)
RES	Log of premiums written in restrictive environments	1.8433[a]	0.0018[a]	0.1519[a]
		(0.2223)	(0.0006)	(0.0130)

		(1)	(2)	(3)
LGROUP	Log of group premiums	0.0049^a	0.0032^b	0.0000
		(0.0008)	(0.0016)	(0.0000)
LLIFE	Log of total U.S. life premiums	0.0049^a	0.0067^a	0.0000
		(0.0008)	(0.0016)	(0.0000)
LAH	Log of total A & H premiums	0.0049^a	0.0020^a	0.0000
		(0.0008)	(0.0004)	(0.0000)
Size	Log of total premiums and annuity considerations	-0.1716^a	-0.0358^b	-0.0154^a
		(0.0269)	(0.0145)	(0.0016)
$Size^2$	Log of total premiums and annuity considerations^2	0.0031^a	0.0004	0.0004^a
		(0.0008)	(0.0004)	(0.0000)
Psuedo R^2		0.35	undefined	0.017
OLS R^2		0.25	0.13	0.26
	Elasticity between Total Licenses and Expense Ratios	0.18	0	0.97

NOTE: Regression weighted by the log of total assets. Standard errors are in parentheses.
a. Significant at the 0.01 level, b. at 0.05 level, c. at 0.1 level.
SOURCE: Author.

suggest increasing returns to scale for the mean firm in the sample. The marginal effect of size in most cases is significantly negative, implying that as size increases, the expense ratio of each category decreases. That evidence of economies of scale is consistent with the results of the insurer efficiency literature (see Cummins and Weiss 1993; Berger, Cummins, and Weiss 1998).

Examining the effect of regulatory environment, we see that writings in restrictive environments (RES) have no significant effect in the property-liability industry. In the life industry, however, the coefficient on RES is significantly positive in every expense ratio regression. The life industry appears to be significantly affected by the restrictive environments.[32]

The number of licenses held by the company significantly affects both industries' expense ratios. Further, if we think of the salary expenses as an indication of the cost of dealing with different regulations among the states, we see that being licensed in more states increases salary expenditures and costs to the insurer.[33] That is true also for the number of license fees paid by the insurer. An increase in the number of regulatory jurisdictions is associated with higher regulatory license fees.[34]

Elasticities can help interpret those results. For example, if the number of state licenses for the mean property-liability firm were to increase by 10 percent, the overall expense ratio would increase by 1 percent, the expense ratio for salaries would increase by 1.4 percent, the claims cost expense ratio would increase by .8 percent, and the expense ratio for fees would increase by .3 percent. For the life industry, we see that a 10 percent increase in states licensed for the mean firm would lead to a 1.8 percent increase in the overall expense ratio, a 0 percent increase in salaries, and a 9.7 percent increase in fees.

A very rough estimate of total regulatory compliance costs would be roughly $4.5 billion, representing less than 1 percent of industry premiums.[35] Readers are advised not to place too much emphasis on that figure, given the preliminary nature of our estimates.

We find evidence of regulatory costs associated with nonessential regulation in the life insurance industry. That is attributable to insurers writing in restrictive regulatory environments. We also find that costs are higher the larger the number of states in which a firm is licensed. To the extent that (1) a federal model will reduce nonessential regulation and (2) nonuniform market conduct regulation across the states increases costs without associated benefits, a federal model might reduce the costs of regulation on the industry.

Conclusions

In sum, we conclude that the potential savings from optional federal chartering depend greatly on the scope and policies of federal regulation and how they would differ from the state regulatory system that may evolve in the future. We argue that there would be some tangible savings from federal regulation, probably small, in the area of solvency or financial regulation. Much larger potential savings could be achieved from delegating market regulatory functions to a federal entity. Even then, the amount of savings in terms of tangible regulatory expenditures and compliance costs could be small relative to industry premiums: less than 1 percent, or $5 billion. Further research could yield smaller or larger estimates of regulatory compliance costs and savings from optional federal chartering.

The intangible costs of regulation in terms of market outcomes are potentially much greater, although they would probably be less affected by the institutional structure of regulation than by the nature of its policies. Significant efficiencies could be achieved under the current state system or under a dual federal-state system by eliminating nonessential market regulations and standardizing those regulations that are retained. Prudential solvency regulation also could significantly reduce intangible market costs. Hence, the scope and design of insurance regulatory policies is probably more important than whether authority resides with the federal government or with the various states. However, one's view of that could be different if structural changes facilitated reforms in regulatory policies. Whichever institutional structure is chosen, the primary focus should be on developing effective and efficient regulatory policies.

Notes

1. See Klein (1995, 1999) for a description of state insurance regulation and recent regulatory initiatives.

2. This chapter differs from analyses of the efficiency of regulators (see Grace and Phillips 1999). Here we attempt to identify the costs of insurance regulation to insurers and consumers.

3. For example, a consumer might purchase a contract that does not adequately cover his risks. If a loss occurs, he might not have the resources to cover the loss. Thus, the consumer faces the possibility of bankruptcy and may externalize his loss to others.

4. Most organizational forms of insurers in the United States limit the liability of owners.

5. The market may attempt to provide information regarding the solvency prospects of the firms in the industry, but that information comes at cost and results in a second-best outcome.

6. In some instances, insurers are allowed to sell certain special types of insurance on a nonlicensed or nonadmitted basis.

7. Over time, guaranty fund coverage of large commercial policyholders has been eliminated in many states, although their premiums are still subject to assessment.

8. Risk-based pricing of assessments or cost-sharing through larger deductibles and co-insurance provisions are other potential measures that could be employed to address the moral hazard problem.

9. About one-half of the states subject personal auto and home insurance to prior-approval rate regulation. A number of states are in the process of eliminating prior-approval requirements for most commercial insurance products. Life insurance prices have generally not been regulated, although the adequacy of benefits is examined in relation to premiums. Regulation of health insurance rates and contract terms appears to be on the rise.

10. Rate suppression distorts price signals to the market and constrains the supply and availability of insurance, and it can increase insolvency risk.

11. Those concerns have prompted the National Conference of Insurance Legislators (NCOIL) to sponsor a study of market-conduct regulation. The use of an applicant's credit history in underwriting auto and home insurance is an example of a contentious issue in market-conduct regulation.

12. The high degree of interdependence among states in regulating multistate insurers is caused by the significant amount of business written in each state by nondomestic companies, as indicated in Klein (1995).

13. See also Meier (1988), Advisory Commission on Intergovernmental Relations (1992), and chapter 2 of this volume for a review of various attempted federal interventions into insurance regulation.

14. For example, when the failure of a number of substandard auto

insurers prompted the introduction of federal legislation to create a national guaranty fund system in 1969, the NAIC moved quickly to adopt model guaranty fund acts for property-casualty and life-health insurers that were subsequently enacted by many states.

15. States can regulate loan rates, and both the federal government and the states have other consumer protection legislation. However, the regulatory or enforcement action tends to come after the fact rather than prior to the release of a product.

16. That is essentially how the FDIC, FSLIC, and state funds operated prior to the savings and loan crisis of the 1980s. There might be a concern that state guaranty associations would be more vulnerable to capacity problems if a large number of insurers opted for federal regulation.

17. See chapter 9 of this volume for a discussion of guaranty association issues involved with federal chartering.

18. Unless indicated otherwise, figures on state insurance departments were obtained from the NAIC's *Insurance Department Resources Report 1997*.

19. Insurance departments are not funded by direct premium taxes on the industry. Premium taxes raised from the industry go to the general fund, where they are allocated to all governmental services. However, some states allow insurance departments to charge fees for regulatory services provided. For example, those would include fees to cover the cost of an insurer's solvency examination.

20. That figure does not include payroll, sales, or property taxes paid by insurance companies to state and local governments.

21. Most state premium tax rates fall in the range of 2 to 3 percent, but various premium tax exclusions and credits reduce effective tax rates below nominal rates.

22. That comparison might be somewhat biased against insurance regulation, as property-liability insurers tend to have fewer assets in relation to the scope of their activities, as compared with life insurers and banks.

23. Property-liability insurers are able to pass a significant portion of guaranty fund assessments to consumers through rate surcharges. Life insurers, however, must rely more heavily on tax credits and deductions because of the long-term nature of life insurance contracts.

24. For example, in some instances, regulators may pressure insurers to pay claims that are not covered under a strict interpretation of their insurance contracts.

25. For the life insurance industry, total premiums include life and health premiums as well as annuity considerations.

26. It is possible that some regulation may actually cause the firm

to make expenditures that are beneficial (in the sense of being profitable) for some insurers. Under regulatory accounting, all expenses are treated equally. However, not all "expenses" are "expenses," as some may be investments with a positive net present value. A better methodology would focus on the profitability of the firm in various environments. This chapter assumes that all regulation imposes costs that do not have any corresponding benefits.

27. In previous years, Conning and Co. did a survey of senior insurance company executives to ask them to rank (or comment on) a state's regulatory environment.

28. The states classified as restrictive are, in rank order, California, Nebraska, Tennessee, Mississippi, New Jersey, North Carolina, Washington, Massachusetts, West Virginia, and Delaware.

29. Our sample has 827 property-liability companies and 1,001 life insurance companies for the year 1997. We excluded companies with ratios of expenses to premiums less than zero or greater than 1 and a ratio of salary expenses to premiums that were less than zero or greater than one. Further, we excluded companies with no assets and those with no premiums.

30. We use the stock dummy as merely a control variable. A large literature has developed to examine the differences among organizational forms. That literature suggests two things. First, stocks and mutuals are equally profitable. They just undertake different strategies to mitigate agency costs. (See, for example, Meyers and Smith 1988.) Second, expense ratios do not account for the multiproduct nature of the firm, nor do they accurately reflect the economic production function underlying the production of insurance. Further, in a case like this, profit functions should be employed to account for the fact that some expenses generate positive benefits. (See, for example, Berger, Cummins, and Weiss 1998.)

31. The same caveat is needed here as in the previous note with regard to the marking arrangement each firm employs (Berger, Cummins, and Weiss 1998).

32. Readers should interpret these regression results with care, as there is multicollinearity among the explanatory variables with some measure of premiums. Some specifications of the property-liability models show significant coefficients on RES.

33. This, as well as the following, discussion assumes that the increased costs can not be passed on to the consumer. Thus the denominator of the expense ratio is constant. That assumption is accurate when and if the individual firm has no ability to raise prices. That would be true in relatively competitive markets, such as the personal lines markets.

34. It should be noted that insurers sometimes have licenses in states in which they are not currently writing any business and, hence, would not be making any rates and forms filings. We attempted to refine that variable by counting the number of states in which a company actively writes business. However, the result was almost identical to that presented here for both the life and property-liability industries.

35. This estimate is based on the assumption that the average cost of being licensed in a state is $100,000 per state, that there are 3,000 companies that write business in multiple states, and that the mean number of licenses per company is fifteen.

References

Advisory Commission on Intergovernmental Relations (ACIR). 1992. *State Solvency Regulation of Property-Casualty and Life Insurance Companies.* Washington, D.C.: Advisory Commission on Intergovernmental Relations.

Berger, Allen J., David Cummins, and Mary A. Weiss. 1998. "The Coexistence of Multiple Distribution Systems for Financial Services: The Case of Property-Liability Insurance." *Journal of Business* 70 (4): 515–46.

Barrese, James, and Jack M. Nelson. 1994. "Some Consequences of Insurer Insolvencies." *Journal of Insurance Regulation* 13: 3–18.

Bohn, James G., and Brian J. Hall. 1998. "The Costs of Insurance Company Failures." In *The Economics of Property-Casualty Insurance,* ed. David F. Bradford. Chicago, Ill.: University of Chicago Press.

Conning and Co. 1997. *1997 State Market Analysis for Property-Casualty Insurance.* Hartford, Conn.: Conning and Co.

Cummins, J. David. 1988. "Risk-Based Premiums for Insurance Guaranty Funds." *Journal of Finance* 43: 823–39.

Cummins, J. David, and Mary A. Weiss. 1991. "The Structure, Conduct, and Regulation of the Property-Liability Insurance Industry." In *The Financial Condition and Regulation of Insurance Companies,* ed. Richard W. Kopcke and Richard E. Randall. Federal Reserve Bank of Boston: 117–54.

———. 1993. "Measuring Cost Efficiency in the Property-Liability Industry." *Journal of Banking and Finance* 17: 463–82.

Grace, Martin F., and Richard D. Phillips. 1999. "The Allocation of Governmental Regulatory Authority: Federalism and the

Case of Insurance Regulation." Center for RMI Research, Georgia State University, WP96–2.

Hall, Brian. 1998. "Risk-Taking Incentives and the Cost of Insurance Company Failures." In *Alternative Approaches to Insurance Regulation,* ed. Robert W. Klein. Kansas City, Mo.: National Association of Insurance Commissioners.

Hanson, Jon S., Robert E. Dineen, and Michael B. Johnson. 1974. *Monitoring Competition: A Means of Regulating the Property and Liability Insurance Business.* Milwaukee, Wis.: NAIC.

Harrington, Scott E. 1992. "Rate Suppression." *Journal of Risk and Insurance* 59: 185–202.

Inman, Robert P., and Daniel Rubinfeld. 1997. "Rethinking Federalism." *Journal of Economic Perspective* 11: 43–64.

Joskow, Paul. 1973. "Cartels, Competition, and Regulation in the Property-Liability Insurance Industry." *Bell Journal of Economics and Management Science* 4: 375–427.

Kimball, Spencer L., and Barbara P. Heaney. 1995. *Federalism and Insurance Regulation: Basic Source Materials.* Kansas City, Mo.: NAIC.

Klein, Robert W. 1995. "Insurance Regulation in Transition." *Journal of Risk and Insurance* 62: 363–404.

———. 1996. "Issues in Financing Insurance Regulation and NAIC Services." Working Paper, National Association of Insurance Commissioners.

———. 1999. *A Regulator's Introduction to the Insurance Industry.* Kansas City, Mo.: National Association of Insurance Commissioners.

Lilly, Claude C. 1976. "A History of Insurance Regulation in the United States." *CPCU Annals* 29: 99–115.

Meier, Kenneth. 1988. *The Political Economy of Regulation: The Case of Insurance.* Albany, N.Y.: SUNY Press.

Meyers, Stewart, and C. Smith. 1988. "Ownership Structure across Lines of Property-Casualty Insurance." *Journal of Law and Economics* 31: 351–78.

Munch, Patricia, and Dennis E. Smallwood. 1981. "Theory of Solvency Regulation in the Property and Casualty Insurance Industry." In *Studies in Public Regulation*, ed. Gary Fromm. Cambridge, Mass.: MIT Press.

National Association of Insurance Commissioners. Various years. *Insurance Department Resource Report.* Kansas City, Mo.: NAIC.

Oates, Wallace. 1972. *Fiscal Federalism.* New York: Harcourt Brace.

Schlesinger, Harris. 1998. "Uncommon Knowledge: Bilateral Asymmetry of Information in Insurance Markets." *Risk Management and Insurance Review* 1 (2): v–ix.

Skipper, Harold D., Jr., ed. 1998. *International Risk and Insurance: An Environmental-Managerial Approach.* Boston, Mass.: Irwin/McGraw-Hill.

Stigler, G. 1971. "The Theory of Economic Regulation." *Bell Journal of Management Science* 3: 3–21.

Spulber, Daniel F. 1989. *Regulation and Markets.* Cambridge, Mass.: MIT Press.

U.S. Congress, House of Representatives, Subcommittee on Oversight and Investigations, House Committee on Energy and Commerce. 1990. *Failed Promises: Insurance Company Insolvencies.* [Dingell Report.] Washington, D.C.: Government Printing Office.

U.S. General Accounting Office. 1989. *Insurance Regulation: Problems in the State Monitoring of Property / Casualty Insurer Solvency.* Washington, D.C.: Government Printing Office.

———. 1991. *Insurance Industry: Questions and Concerns about Solvency Regulation.* Statement of Johnny C. Finch before the Committee on Commerce, Science and Transportation, U.S. Senate. Washington, D.C.: Government Printing Office.

Varian, Hal R. 1992. *Microeconomic Analysis.* New York, N.Y.: W.W. Norton.

PART FIVE

Regulatory Issues—The Devil Is in the Details

9

The Fate of the State Guaranty Funds after the Advent of Federal Insurance Chartering

Bert Ely

There is a growing likelihood that Congress will authorize the federal chartering of insurance companies as an alternative to state insurance chartering. This chapter addresses the issue of protecting the insureds of federally chartered insurance companies and third-party claimants of those companies under liability policies against any loss of their insurance coverage, should a federally chartered insurance company become insolvent. The second section of this chapter will frame that issue, and the third will describe the state guaranty funds that have provided insolvency protection for state-chartered insurance companies, up to specified dollar limits.

The fourth section of the chapter will discuss similarities and, more important, differences between the state guaranty funds and federal deposit insurance. That comparison is important because federal deposit insurance will provide Congress with an important point of reference in designing a system for protecting the insureds and third-party claimants of federally chartered insurance companies. The fifth section will discuss eight important policy questions Congress must address in designing a protection mechanism for federally chartered insurers. A second point of reference for that design will be legislation that Representative John Dingell (D-Michigan) introduced in 1992 and 1993 that would have created a Federal Insurance Solvency Commission. The final section of the chapter will describe the

cross-guarantee concept for privatizing banking regulation and
its attendant financial risks, and how that concept can be extended
to provide protection for insureds and third-party claimants
of federally chartered insurers.

Framing the Issue

If Congress decides to authorize the federal chartering of insurance
companies, it will be faced with a fundamental question—
what obligation will the federal government have toward the
insureds, third-party claimants, and other creditors of federally
chartered insurance companies? That is the same question that
state legislatures have faced for decades in chartering and regulating
state-chartered insurance companies.

In addressing that question, Congress almost certainly will
slide down the same slippery slope as did the states in establishing
the state guaranty funds, based on the following logic. Insurance
is the kind of business, like banking, in which there is a
strong public policy interest in preventing the insolvency of insurance
companies in order to protect the insureds and third-party
claimants of those companies. That is, government wants
insurance companies to be highly reliable sources of insurance
protection, particularly for individuals and small businesses. As
one commentator has observed:

> Because banks, insurance companies, and related financial
> intermediaries play an important role in the financial
> security of the citizenry, the government has a
> strong interest in assuring their soundness and in preventing
> the kinds of systemic failures that led to financial
> devastation in the [Great] Depression.[1]

Therefore, to ensure the solvency of federally chartered insurance
companies, Congress almost certainly will enact, as a
key component of federal insurance chartering legislation, a set
of rules designed to minimize the occurrence of insolvency among
federally chartered insurers and to quickly put out of business
those insurers chartered under federal law that are sliding
toward insolvency.

Those rules will be enforced by a government agency, most
likely the issuer of insurance charters. That agency will issue

insurance solvency regulations, periodically examine the federally chartered insurers, supervise them, and, under procedures akin to the prompt corrective action (PCA) rules enacted by the Federal Deposit Insurance Corporation Improvement Act of 1991 (FDICIA), will close and liquidate or sell failing insurance companies. Anyone familiar with federal banking law and regulation will quickly recognize the many parallels that will exist with federal insurance regulation. Complaints about federal insurance regulation will sound remarkably similar to complaints about federal banking regulation.

If insurance regulation, like banking regulation, worked perfectly, then failing insurance companies would be resolved before they became insolvent. In that circumstance, there would be no need for insurance guarantee protections, just as there would be no need for deposit insurance. Insureds and claimants, like bank depositors, would never suffer a loss or delay in receiving payment. But, alas, insurance regulators, like bank regulators, are far from perfect—hundreds of insurance companies have failed in recent decades, with substantial insolvency losses that would have been borne by insureds and claimants had it not been for the state guaranty funds. For example, the net loss (payouts and administrative expenses minus recoveries) of the state property-and-casualty (P&C) guaranty funds for the 1969–1997 period was $6.5 billion.[2] The net loss for the state life and health (L&H) guaranty funds, in multistate insolvencies only, for the 1990–1998 period was $4.45 billion.[3] While not insignificant, those are modest amounts compared with the $160 billion cost of the S&L crisis.

Although not widely recognized as such, the state guaranty funds, like federal deposit insurance (FDI), represent a product warranty. Specifically, the states have created a mechanism (the state guaranty funds) that protects innocent third parties (insureds and third-party insurance claimants) against regulatory negligence and failure on the part of state-employed insurance regulators. In effect, the state guaranty funds, like FDI, reflect this political reality: if government wants to be in the business, for whatever reason, of regulating financial institutions, then it has no choice but to provide a warranty for the service that business supposedly provides to the general public.[4] That proposition can be viewed from another perspective—if government is not liable for its regulatory negligence, then what is the point of having government regulation in the first place?

Just as the states provide a product warranty for their insurance regulation, in the form of the state guaranty funds, and just as the federal government provides a product warranty for its banking regulation, through FDI, so too will Congress feel compelled to provide a product warranty for its regulation of federally chartered insurance companies. Major questions will arise, though, as to how the product warranty will be specified, how warranty losses will be minimized, and who will pay for those losses. Initially, the state guaranty funds will coexist with a federal insurance product warranty; that is, a federal insurance guarantee, or FIG. However, just as nonfederal deposit insurance, with two exceptions,[5] could not compete successfully against FDI, one must wonder how long the state guaranty funds will be able to compete against a FIG. Victor Palmieri, chairman and CEO of the Palmieri Company and the receiver in several major insurance insolvency cases, observed after envisioning a federal insurance charter that:

> This would leave smaller, less capitalized insurers under state regulation. This dual system will likely result in new strains for the guaranty association system because of the reduced assessment capacity of state guaranty associations as the largest companies opt for federal regulation.[6]

The Background of the State Guaranty Funds

As with deposit insurance, the state guaranty funds sprang from adversity, in particular from the failure of more than one hundred "high-risk" auto insurers in the 1960–1969 period. As a result of those failures, several bills were introduced in the Senate in the 1960s to establish a federal insurance or guaranty mechanism to protect the insureds and third-party claimants of failed insurance companies. In May 1969, Senator Warren Magnuson (D-Washington) introduced a bill (S. 2236) to create a Federal Insurance Guaranty Corporation (FIGC) that would have provided insolvency protection for virtually all lines of P&C insurance. Within a month, the National Association of Insurance Commissioners (NAIC) began work on a model State Post-Insolvency Assessment Insurance Guaranty Association Act for P&C insurers.

By the end of 1971, most states had enacted some version of that model, thereby creating the state guaranty funds. Today, all states have guaranty funds for their P&C insurers. All of them, with one exception, operate on a post-assessment basis; that is, they assess surviving insurers for losses in failed insurance companies as those losses are paid. New York is the sole exception—it operates a pre-assessment system, with the insurance companies assessed only when there is a need to replenish the state fund.

A similar state guaranty fund system to protect the insureds of insolvent L&H insurance companies emerged more slowly, largely because of opposition from the life insurance industry. Consequently, it took until 1983 for thirty-four states to enact guaranty association laws for their L&H insurers.[7] Not until 1992 had all states enacted guaranty association legislation for their L&H insurers.[8]

Because many insurance companies, including all the larger ones, have long operated on a multistate, if not national, basis, the guaranty funds, working through the NAIC and the two national associations of guaranty funds, have developed procedures for managing the loss payouts of failed multistate insurers. Those associations are the National Conference of Insurance Guaranty Funds for P&C insurers and the National Organization of Life and Health Insurance Guaranty Associations (NOLHGA).

The creation of the state guaranty funds enabled the insurance industry and the NAIC to fend off federal intervention in an important aspect of the insurance industry: the protection of insureds and third-party claimants. However, the spate of insurance company failures in the 1980s and early 1990s prompted Representative John Dingell, then chairman and now ranking Democrat on the powerful House Commerce Committee, to introduce in 1992 and again in 1993 a bill entitled the Federal Insurance Solvency Act (H.R. 1290 in 1993). That bill would have created a Federal Insurance Solvency Commission that would establish and enforce uniform national standards for all insurers operating in interstate commerce. As a practical matter, the bill would have established federal regulation for all multistate insurers. The Dingell bill also would have federalized the regulation of the reinsurance industry. Finally, the bill would have established the National Insurance Protection Corporation (NIPC) to protect the insureds of any insolvent insurer regulated by the federal government. The operation of the NIPC would have been modeled on the structure, procedures, and requirements of the Securities Investor Protection Corporation.[9]

Similarities and Differences between the State Guaranty Funds and Federal Deposit Insurance

There are important similarities and differences between the state guaranty funds and FDI that will have a strong bearing on the construction of a FIG for federally chartered insurers.

Limits on the scope of protection are perhaps the greatest similarity between the guaranty funds and FDI. However, while FDI has a fairly simple and widely advertised limit—$100,000 per depositor, per bank[10]—the guaranty fund limits are more complex and they vary from state to state. For example, there might be one limit on the refund of unearned premiums, a separate limit on loss claims, and other limitations and exclusions, such as excluding coverage on punitive damage claims, or for insureds with a net worth exceeding a stated amount. The other key similarity is that survivors in the industry, presumably the better capitalized and managed firms, are taxed to pay for regulatory failure, specifically the failure of regulators to promptly close those firms that the regulators have not prevented from becoming insolvent.

The differences between the state guaranty funds and FDI, however, are significant in two respects that will have an important bearing on how Congress resolves the issue of protecting the insureds and third-party claimants of federally chartered insurers. First, Congress may find certain aspects of the state funds unacceptable for ensuring the protection of the insureds and third-party claimants of federally chartered insurance companies. Second, Congress may reject various aspects of state guaranty fund operation in constructing a FIG and its administrative apparatus. The following are the key differences.

Fund Administration. The state guaranty funds are nonprofit associations of all companies licensed to write insurance within a state in the lines of insurance covered by the guaranty fund. Insurance companies therefore are required to belong to a state's guaranty fund in order to obtain a license to sell insurance in that state. The board of directors of each guaranty fund is composed of representatives from member companies and from the state insurance commissioner's office.[11] Sometimes there is a public member or two on those boards. Overall, though, there is a close working relationship between the insurance industry and its regulators. That is quite different from FDI, which is run as an integral component of federal banking regulation, or from the operation of the Federal Insurance Solvency Commission that would have been created under the Dingell legislation.

Fund Balance, or Lack Thereof. With the exception of New York's pre-assessment system, the state guaranty funds are not funds in the sense that they have fund balances from which losses are paid. Instead, loss payments are assessed on surviving insurers as those losses are paid. Under FDI, however, there is no direct linkage between the occurrence of losses (when the existence of a loss is first recognized by the regulators) and the payment of a loss. The Dingell bill envisioned the creation of a fund balance in the NIPC comparable to the fund balances that exist in the FDIC's two insurance funds, the Bank Insurance Fund (BIF) and the Savings Association Insurance Fund (SAIF). However, as a practical matter, the two fund balances are fictions, since they are treated as part of the consolidated federal budget. Further, any decline in either fund below a 1.25 percent reserve ratio (the fund's balance as a percentage of insured deposits) must quickly be offset with higher deposit insurance premiums. That requirement effectively means that the bottom portion of a fund balance, up to 1.25 percent of insured deposits, is *not* available to absorb bank or thrift insolvency losses, except over the short term.

Product Line Differentiations. Unlike deposit insurance, which does not differentiate between types of deposits (checking versus savings) or types of domestic depositors (individual versus large corporation),[12] the state guaranty funds have various product divisions. The guaranty funds divide into two broad categories—P&C and L&H. Within those two categories are subdivisions such as workers' compensation, automobile, and all other P&C lines, or life, health, and annuities; those subdivisions vary from state to state. Also, certain forms of insurance, such as title insurance, are often excluded from guaranty fund protection. The Dingell bill would have had six subdivisions within the NIPC, and yet it also listed thirteen exclusions from any NIPC protection at all.

Coverage Limits. As noted above, coverage limits vary from state to state, up to $500,000, by type of insurance product, and by type of liability (prepaid premiums versus actual loss, cash values versus life insurance death benefits, and so forth). For FDI, there is one nationwide insurance limit—$100,000 per depositor, per bank.

Who Ultimately Pays for Insolvency Losses. One of the major differences between FDI and the state guaranty funds is the extent to which losses are contained within the affected industry. With the significant exception of the taxpayer bailout of the Federal Savings and Loan Insurance Corporation, depository institutions have paid for FDI losses through deposit insurance premiums. Further, numerous reforms that Congress has enacted since 1989 have effectively eliminated the taxpayer risk previously posed by FDI.[13] Treatment of guaranty fund assessments, however, varies significantly among the states, with many states permitting insurers to reduce the premium taxes they pay by the amount of the guaranty fund assessments they pay.[14]

Premium tax offsets permit surviving insurance companies to pass the cost of insurance company failures through to general taxpayers. More states permit L&H insurers to offset fund assessments against premium taxes than is the case with assessments against P&C insurers because L&H insurers cannot pass their assessments through to owners of existing long-term life insurance contracts. The Dingell bill did not provide any such offset, possibly because insurance companies do not pay premium taxes to the federal government.

Risk Sensitivity of Premiums. One of the surprising shortcomings of the state guaranty funds, given that insurance companies are supposed to factor risk into the premiums they charge, is the complete lack of risk sensitivity in state guaranty fund assessments. That lack at least partially reflects their ex post, or after-the-fact, nature. Although Congress, through FDICIA, tried to push the FDIC toward levying risk-sensitive premiums, the FDIC has not been very successful in developing genuinely risk-sensitive premiums: that is, premiums that are based on leading measures of banking risk and are intended to deter banks from unwise risk-taking. Interestingly, when the FDIC in early 1999 attempted to introduce more risk into its premiums, it quickly had to back down because of political opposition.[15]

Public Policy Questions Congress Must Address

Operating on the fairly safe assumption that Congress will insist on protecting insureds and third-party claimants from the insolvency of federally chartered insurance companies, Congress will have to address a number of questions regarding the nature and provision of that coverage. Although many of those issues were addressed in the 1993 Dingell bill, it is useful to review them, particularly in light of the financial services modernization legislation Congress enacted in 1999 (S. 900). Those issues include:

Whether or not to provide federal insolvency protection for the insureds of federally chartered insurers. The threshold question that Congress must address in creating a federal insurance charter is how to provide for the insolvency protection of the insureds and third-party claimants of federally chartered insurers. One option would be to rely on the existing system of state guaranty funds to provide that protection, including the existing mechanism for dealing with the insolvency of multistate insurers. However, Congress might be troubled by the lack of uniformity of guaranty fund protections across the states. If Congress were so troubled, it might then insist on a uniform standard of protection, which would put many of the guaranty funds in the position of operating with different levels of protection for state and federally chartered insurers, or having to adopt the federal standard for its state-chartered members.

Congress also would be concerned with the assessment capacity of the state guaranty funds, since there would be, in light of Congress's bailout of the FSLIC, a fairly explicit federal guarantee of the insolvency protection provided for the insureds and third-party claimants of federally chartered insurers. Given those complexities and the precedent set by the two Dingell bills, Congress probably would opt to create a FIG for federally chartered insurance companies.

Admission of state-chartered insurance companies into the FIG program. If Congress does create a FIG and a federal agency to administer that guarantee, then Congress will have to immediately address the question of whether or not to admit state-chartered insurers into the program in the same manner that the FDIC has always been open to state-chartered banks. However, just as Congress broadly extended federal safety-and-soundness regulation to state-chartered, federally insured banks and thrifts in the aftermath of the S&L crisis, so too would it reasonably take the same approach toward state-chartered but federally guaranteed insurers. That approach reflects the fact that he who insures must, of necessity, also regulate in order to minimize losses. The failure in 1999 of seven insurance companies controlled by Martin Frankel raised anew long-standing concerns about the quality of state insurance regulation; losses in the Frankel fiasco may exceed $200 million.[16] What is especially troubling is that Tennessee insurance examiners had been suspicious about the activities of one of the Frankel-controlled insurance companies since 1993.[17]

Admission of state-chartered insurers into a FIG program would then create not only dual chartering for insurers, but also a dual guaranty mechanism that did not exist in the banking industry when the FDIC was created (all state deposit insurers had failed by 1933). Further, very limited nonfederal deposit insurance for S&Ls and credit unions emerged after World War II, so there never has been significant competition between state-chartered insurers and the federal government in the deposit insurance arena. Given that nonfederal deposit insurance has almost entirely disappeared, it is reasonable to speculate that the state guaranty funds would soon start to wither if state-chartered insurers could become federally guaranteed, as the Dingell bill envisioned.

Relationship of the FIG program to the FDIC. Although the Dingell bill envisioned an NIPC that would be independent of the FDIC, that independence must be questioned in light of the convergence of banking and insurance, as reflected in the financial services modernization legislation Congress enacted in 1999. Further, given the many similarities between the FDIC's mission as a deposit insurer (as differentiated from its mission as a banking regulator) and the mission of the federal agency administering the FIG Fund, a strong argument can be made that all forms of federal financial insolvency protection (including credit union share insurance), as well as the resolution of failed financial institutions, should be administered by one federal agency. The federal resolution of insolvent, federally guaranteed insurers would represent a significant change from the existing, expensive state system for resolving insolvent insurers. According to one estimate, for every one dollar of assets in insolvent P&C companies, liquidators turn over an average of only 33 cents to the guaranty funds.[18] Asset recovery rates generally are much higher in failed institutions insured by the FDIC.

The argument for having just one federal insolvency insurer/resolution agency was strengthened by the 1999 financial services modernization legislation, which permits banks and insurers to affiliate within a holding company structure. Although that legislation strengthened the obsolete notion of functional regulation, Congress may be reluctant to extend the functional regulation concept to creditor protection if it creates a FIG program.

Fund balance in a FIG Fund. Although there is no logical relationship between a deposit insurance fund balance and the insolvency risks which that fund faces, the concept of a deposit insurance fund balance has become well embedded at the federal level, partly because it is fairly easy to compute a desired fund balance—simply multiply some measure of bank deposits (usually an estimate of insured deposits) by an arbitrary percentage. Life is not so easy in the insurance arena, though, because liabilities to insureds and third-party claimants are not easily measured, particularly for P&C companies and especially for their long-tail liabilities. Natural disasters, which strike suddenly and, often, fatally for small P&C insurers, create another major uncertainty in determining an appropriate fund balance. There-fore, assuming that Congress will want the FIG Fund to have some sort of advanced funding, it will have to determine how that fund balance will be calculated. The Dingell bill left that determination to the directors of the NIPC.

Emergency access to the Fed discount window. Theoretically, insurance companies, like securities firms, can borrow from the Federal Reserve's discount window in "unusual and exigent cir-cumstances"; that is, if they are experiencing severe liquidity problems. However, unlike banks, which can borrow at the dis-count window of a Federal Reserve Bank without prior approval of the Board of Governors of the Federal Reserve System, loans to nonbank firms, such as insurance companies, require an af-firmative vote of five members of the Board of Governors.[19] Un-published reports suggest that there have been times, specifically in the mid-1970s and the late 1980s, when insurance companies suffering liquidity problems approached the Fed about borrowing at the discount window, but were rebuffed by the Fed. According to NOLHGA, the July 1991 failure of the Mu-tual Benefit Life Insurance Company, a $13 billion insurer, cre-ated a classic "run-on-the-bank" scenario, in part "because Mutual Benefit's pension plan–held contracts did not have very restrictive withdrawal provisions."[20]

Although not widely seen as a problem, a run on a life in-surer in particular can create a much longer term liquidity prob-lem for that company than troubled banks usually experience, since people return to banks more quickly, in order to manage their liquidity, than they will return to a life insurer. P&C insur-ers facing substantial claims after a major natural catastrophe also can face liquidity problems. If Congress creates a FIG pro-gram, it almost certainly will want to liberalize the access that federally guaranteed insurers have to the Fed's discount window. That would give the FIG program a significant competitive ad-vantage over the state guaranty funds.

Product line coverages and exclusions/coverage limits. One of the most important determinations Congress will have to make in creating a FIG program will be determining who will be protected by the FIG, what types of insurance coverages and insureds will *not* be protected, and the amount of coverage. That problem will be made more complex by the substantial exposure that many P&C companies have to natural disasters such as hurricanes, floods, and earthquakes. Although the states have regulated many of the insurances that have not been subject to state guaranty fund protection, it is an open question as to whether or not Congress will be comfortable with such exclusions for federally chartered insurers, and specifically with the range of exclusions specified in the Dingell bill. If there is any aspect of the federal chartering of insurance companies where the devil is in the details, it certainly will lie in defining the coverages, coverage amounts, and exclusions under a FIG program and in dealing with catastrophic risk exposures.

FIG premiums. Given its extensive experience with FDI, it is unlikely that Congress, in creating a FIG program, will adopt the relatively simplistic post-insolvency loss assessment procedures of the state guaranty funds. First, it probably will insist on some degree of prefunding for a FIG Fund, as did the Dingell bill. Second, it probably will want an attempt made to incorporate risk-sensitivity into FIG Fund premiums. Third, it will expect the FIG Fund to be entirely self-sufficient, even during times of great economic distress, as it now expects for FDI. That requirement will be especially tough on life insurers because they would not be able to pass premium increases through on existing policies that account for most of their insurance liabilities. A taxpayer bailout of the FIG Fund will be highly unacceptable to Congress, as will any delay in FIG payments attributable to an annual assessment cap common to the state guaranty funds. Fourth, it will have to categorize the broad range of insurance products for the purpose of determining separate assessment rates for each category.

The federal chartering/guarantee challenge. The federal chartering of insurance companies is becoming increasingly likely because of the growing inefficiencies associated with the highly balkanized state regulation of insurance. However, determining the means for protecting insureds and third-party claimants against insurance company insolvencies may present the toughest set of issues Congress will have to address when authorizing a federal insurance charter. In part because of its experience with FDI, Congress most likely will *not* emulate the structure and operation of the state guaranty funds when creating a mechanism for protecting the insureds and third-party claimants of federally chartered insurance companies.

While the 1993 Dingell bill provides one road map for providing that protection, that bill did not provide for federal chartering of insurance companies, although it did envision establishing a strong federal influence over the regulation of state-chartered, multistate insurers. The issue of protecting the insureds and third-party claimants of federally chartered insurers may therefore become both the Achilles' heel and the briar patch of federal insurance chartering. That possibility suggests that fresh, radical thinking should be applied to the federal chartering/guarantee issue.

The Cross-Guarantee Alternative for a Federal Insurance Guarantee

One approach to a federal-level guarantee fund would be the 100 percent cross-guarantee concept, which has been proposed for privatizing banking regulation and its attendant deposit insurance, too-big-to-fail, and systemic risks.[21] Representative Tom Petri (R-Wisconsin) has introduced legislation on several occasions, most recently in 1996 as H.R. 4318, which would implement the cross-guarantee concept.

Despite contrary impressions, the cross-guarantee concept represents a modest departure from the present system of FDI and government banking regulation as well as the state guaranty funds and state insurance regulation. Essentially, all the cross-guarantee concept does is (1) delegate the safety-and-soundness regulation of individual banks and insurance companies to the *direct*, private-sector guarantors of each guaranteed institution's guaranteed liabilities; (2) explicitly extend the too-big-to-fail (TBTF) concept to all banks and insurers; (3) further strengthen the already substantial taxpayer protections of FDI. Central to the cross-guarantee concept is the notion that the protection of depositors and insureds should *not* be viewed as social insurance funded by general tax revenues. Instead, that protective activity should be viewed as a business, just as P&C and L&H insurance have long been viewed.

The first step in implementing a cross-guarantee system is

to introduce marketplace democracy by giving individual banks and insurers the freedom to decide which institutions they will help to guarantee and which ones they will not guarantee. In return for providing that guarantee, those guarantors will charge a contractually specified, risk-sensitive premium (discussed below) as well as appoint a private-sector firm, called a "syndicate agent," to ensure that the guaranteed institution (bank, thrift institution, or insurance company) complies with the negotiated safety-and-soundness provisions of the cross-guarantee contract (also discussed below). Once a contract takes effect, the guaranteed institution will be exempt from *all* government safety-and-soundness regulation. Therefore, it will be exempt from all government safety-and-soundness oversight; that will become the sole responsibility of the institution's guarantors and their syndicate agent. As a result of that voluntary contracting process, those guarantors directly at risk in bank or insurance company failures will be able to optimize that risk, through negotiated premium rates and contractual restrictions, thereby eliminating one of the great shortcomings of FDI and the state guaranty funds—their systemwide mutualization of losses.

One of the great virtues of privatizing banking and insurance regulation, or more specifically, delegating it to guarantors and their syndicate agents, is that it will permit banks and insurers to escape one-size-must-fit-all regulation, an inherent characteristic of government regulation, state or federal. Instead, each guaranteed bank or insurance company, working with a syndicate agent, will negotiate with its syndicate of direct guarantors only those safety-and-soundness requirements that are logical for that bank's or insurer's business strategy. In effect, a bank or insurance company would negotiate contractual terms, including premium rates, that fit its business strategy. More diversified strategies will result, leading to a sounder financial services industry.

Perhaps the most important element in a cross-guarantee contract would be the formula for periodically computing its risk-sensitive cross-guarantee premium; under the formula, the premium rate might be adjusted as often as monthly or even weekly. As with other provisions in a cross-guarantee contract, the factors in the formula would be negotiated by the guaranteed bank or insurance company with its direct guarantors. The periodic adjustment of premium rates under those formulas would discourage sudden increases in a bank or insurance company's risk appetite. In effect, the keen risk sensitivity of cross-guarantee premium formulas will become a powerful deterrent to risky banking and insurance practices, a deterrent now absent in FDI premiums or state guaranty fund assessments. The marketplace tailoring of premium formulas to individual business strategies will have an important side benefit—the cross-subsidies that now plague FDI and the state guaranty funds will be minimized.

Thus, the cross-guarantee concept, although developed initially for use in the banking industry, can easily be extended to protect the insureds of federally chartered insurance companies.

Conclusion

The time is fast approaching when Congress will authorize the federal chartering of insurance companies, as the present balkanization of state insurance regulation increasingly hobbles that industry. Politically, increasing segments of the insurance industry favor a federal chartering option so that the insurance industry will have a dual chartering option that has long been available to banking. However, the protection of the insureds and third-party claimants of federally chartered insurance companies remains a seldom discussed aspect of federal insurance chartering. Yet this aspect of federal insurance chartering may be one of the most difficult to accomplish, largely because of the manner in which the state guaranty funds have evolved over the past three decades.

Separately, Congress is struggling with other issues: deposit insurance reform; the growing obsolescence of functional regulation, attributable to the melding of all types of financial services products and firms; and the emergence of threats to the federal financial safety net *outside* of the banking industry, as the Long Term Capital Management caper demonstrated in 1998. That melding process will accelerate the growth of large, globally active financial conglomerates offering a broad range of banking, insurance, and securities products. The challenge that policymakers face was acknowledged by one NOLHGA official when he wrote:

It is increasingly apparent that convergence in the financial services industry is a fact of life. What is not quite so apparent is the regulatory framework in which these industry giants will work.[22]

The cross-guarantee concept for privatizing banking and insurance regulation and its attendant financial risks would facilitate financial services modernization by eliminating the need for regulatorily differentiating financial products and firms. More specifically, it would facilitate federal insurance chartering by resolving, in a highly satisfactory manner, the surprisingly thorny problem of providing for the protection of insureds and third-party claimants of federally chartered insurers. In fact, pulling banks and insurance companies into the same cross-guarantee system would go a long way toward eliminating the increasingly unnecessary need to regulatorily differentiate banks from insurance companies.

Notes

1. David A. Skeel, Jr., "The Law and Finance of Bank and Insurance Insolvency Regulation," *Texas Law Review* 76 (4) (March 1998): 723–80.
2. "Financial Information, 01/01/69 to 12/31/97" (table), National Conference of Insurance Guarantee Funds, Indianapolis, Indiana, September 1998.
3. Figure obtained from the National Organization of Life and Health Insurance Guaranty Associations.
4. The author discusses the notion of deposit insurance as a product warranty more fully in "Regulatory Moral Hazard: The Real Moral Hazard in Federal Deposit Insurance," *The Independent Review: A Journal of Political Economy* (Fall 1999).
5. The first of the two exceptions comprises the American Share Insurance Company of Dublin, Ohio, and its wholly owned subsidiary, the Excess Share Insurance Corporation. The first company provides deposit insurance for several hundred state-chartered credit unions *not* insured by the federal government's National Credit Union Share Insurance Fund. The second company provides excess deposit insurance coverage, up to $250,000, for federally insured credit unions. The second exception is the Kansas Bankers Surety Company of Topeka, Kansas, which offers excess deposit insurance to small banks.
6. Victor Palmieri, as quoted in Peter Marigliano, " 'Convergence' of Banks, Insurers May Cause Headaches for Guaranty Associations,"

NOLHGA Journal [National Organization of Life and Health Guaranty Associations] 5 (1) (Winter 1998): 4.

7. "NOLHGA and the Evolution of the State Guaranty Association System," *NOLHGA Journal* (May 1997): 17.

8. Ibid., 5.

9. Representative John Dingell, "Congressional Record—Extension of Remarks," March 10, 1993: E557–59.

10. Two or more depositors can, however, obtain multiples of the $100,000 insurance limit in a bank by varying how they legally title their accounts in that bank.

11. James G. Bohn and Brian J. Hall, "The Moral Hazard of Insuring the Insurers," National Bureau of Economics Research, Inc., Cambridge, Mass., Working Paper 5911 (January 1997): 4.

12. Depositors in foreign branches of U.S. banks are not protected against loss unless their bank is declared to be too-big-to-fail under FDICIA's systemic risk exception (12 U.S.C. Sec. 1823(c)(4)(G)).

13. Those reforms are discussed in a paper by the author, "Banks Do *Not* Receive a Federal Safety Net Subsidy," Financial Services Roundtable, Washington, D.C., May 1999: 6–8.

14. According to various sources, P&C insurers can offset guaranty fund assessments to some extent in at least seventeen states; for L&H insurers, premium tax offsets are permitted in at least thirty-seven states.

15. Scott Barancik, "FDIC Is Developing a System to Make Some Well-Capitalized Banks Pay More," *American Banker* (January 4, 1999): 2; Scott Barancik, "FDIC Puts Off Charging Banks More," *American Banker* (February 16, 1999): 4.

16. Deborah Lohse and Leslie Scism, "Scandal's Toll May Be Sliced to $215 Million," *Wall Street Journal* (June 30, 1999).

17. Scot J. Paltrow, "Tennessee Insurance Official Quits amid Frankel-Related Inquiry," *Wall Street Journal* (August 9, 1999).

18. Brian J. Hall, "Regulatory Free Cash Flow and the High Cost of Insurance Company Failures," Harvard University Graduate School of Business, Boston, Mass., unpublished paper, August 1998: 2–3.

19. 12 U.S.C. Sec. 343, second paragraph.

20. "NOLHGA and the Evolution of the State Guaranty Association System," National Organization of Life and Health Insurance Guaranty Associations (May 1997): 37–38.

21. The cross-guarantee concept is discussed at greater length in Tom Petri and Bert Ely, "Better Banking for America: The 100 Percent Cross-Guarantee Solution," *Common Sense* (Fall 1995): 96–112. Other articles and papers on the cross-guarantee concept are posted on the Ely & Company website at http://www.ely-co.com.

22. Marigliano, "Headaches for Guaranty Associations": 5.

10

Creating Federal Insurance Regulation: A Zero-Based Approach

Robert C. Eager and Cantwell F. Muckenfuss III

Remarks by Robert C. Eager

The impetus for creating this book about federal regulation of insurance is the growing sense that a federal platform for insurance is needed for competitive reasons in a national—indeed, international—marketplace. Despite recurring calls for reform, deregulation under the existing system has been inadequate in fundamental ways. Within the financial-services industry at the end of the twentieth century, insurance alone is subject to significant regulation based on the nature of the product, its price, and the state in which it is delivered.

The state system is not demonstrably broken, but clearly it suffers from major problems. With a few exceptions, state insurance departments are increasingly regarded as unsophisticated, understaffed, slow, and costly. New forms and products must be cleared under each state's laws and rules. Similarly, each state must license each provider and agent doing business in that state. Multistate mechanisms to facilitate interstate insurance operations do not exist. The state-only system is not capable of serving the needs of interstate or nationwide providers of insurance.

The goal in the creation of an optional federal charter is to create a platform for the conduct of insurance business in the global competitive environment of the future. To replicate the existing state system at the federal level makes no sense. We can and should develop a federal charter that embodies contemporary insights about regulation, market dynamics, and best practices in general.

Although winds of change are now evident, the insurance industry has been staunchly committed to exclusive state regulation for a very long time. That commitment is deeply ingrained intellectually and politically—and emotionally as well—both within the industry and among state insurance commissioners. An effort to enact a federal charter and regulation thus will be a political task of historic proportions. This is clearly a long-term project, and it may require an actual or perceived crisis to propel a bill to final passage by Congress.

Those political considerations have several implications. First, the very absence of a crisis should allow a more dispassionate and careful discussion of the issues and options. There may be the luxury of time to get it right. Second, a crisis atmosphere tends to focus attention on dealing with the symptoms, as well as the causes, of the crisis. These concerns often drive legislation and override other considerations. The thrift and banking industries are still living with a number of ill-considered, and in some instances wrong-headed, provisions enacted in the two major bills responding to the S&L debacle and the wave of bank failures in the 1980s. Third, a proposal emerging from a thorough debate outside of Congress should be better crafted and more difficult to attack politically than one that has been hastily assembled in response to a perceived political opening.

Political reality dictates that a federal charter be optional and create a dual state-federal insurance system. That is desirable because, as Mr. Muckenfuss will suggest, there is real virtue to a system that fosters competition through choice. The present dual banking system is a relevant model and on the whole demonstrates the competitive and regulatory vitality of a dual system.

Indeed, I think we have already seen in the insurance area how a dual system can have positive effects. The mere introduction of the Brooke bill in the 1970s and of the Dingell bill in the early 1990s were wake-up calls to the states that had positive effects. The National Association of Insurance Commissioners (NAIC) and the state insurance regulators made very significant strides to improve the state system in the past decade, and it strikes me that at least part of their motivation resulted from the introduction of federal legislation that could have major implications for the way insurance is regulated.

Beyond that example, the dual banking system is relevant as a starting point, and on some issues a foil, with respect to how a federal insurance statute and regulatory agency should be constructed. Two decades ago the Ford administration Justice Department conducted a study that concluded that insurance regulation ought to be reformed and that the dual banking system was an appropriate model. The tendency of such a system to foster deregulation was cited in support of that conclusion. The analysis and conclusions of that study were reflected in the 1976 Brooke bill proposing creation of a federal insurance agency. (That bill stands as the only bill to propose a federal insurance charter, but it largely adopted existing banking or insurance models.)

We agree that the dual banking model can be useful as a reference point, but we do not think it should be imported wholesale any more than one would import wholesale from the existing state regulatory system. Each of the many issues needs to be considered separately. We strongly believe that a zero-base approach should be taken, picking and choosing among conceptual alternatives and best practices.

The list of topics is indeed a long agenda. For now, let me tick off a number of the issues and help to set a framework.

Scope of a Federal Charter. A threshold question is whether to create a comprehensive, full-blown federal charter that provides federal regulation across the board, or to have the federal charter cover only certain matters and leave federally chartered insurers still subject to certain parts of state law. The latter approach would create a mixed system that would include federal elements and also preserve and build on parts of the state system. A further issue is whether the federal regulator alone should enforce compliance with those areas of state law, or whether the relevant state insurance regulator should have that authority.

Preemption. Closely related is the question of the scope of federal preemption. A number of models exist in the banking industry. Two are similar but have an important difference—the national bank and the federal thrift.

The National Bank Act was adopted in a context somewhat similar to what we have with insurance—that is, a federal law created in a context of a well-established and functioning state system. This act provides substantial, but not complete, federal preemption. It preempts only in areas where there is a conflict between state and federal regulation, where state regulation gets in the way of achieving the federal objective.

The federal thrift charter, by contrast, preempts the field. In the 1930s, Congress directed the then Federal Home Loan Bank Board, now the Office of Thrift Supervision (OTS), to create a thrift charter and administer a federal thrift system. Since then, the courts have upheld the notion that anything within the purview of federal thrift regulation is solely a federal matter, even in areas where federal regulation may be silent. In such areas, federal thrifts may be subject to no regulation because state regulation in that area may be preempted.

I would note that the scope of that preemption has been one of the reasons why the federal thrift charter has proved so attractive to the many insurance companies that have applied for thrift charters in the past few years. Some of those companies have recognized that the federal thrift charter and its capacity to operate efficiently on a nationwide basis, including over the Internet, can provide a kind of glue to help them develop and cement relations with their existing insurance customer base. The preemptive federal thrift charter is seen as a key part of a national platform for providing insurance and other nonbanking financial products and services, even under today's balkanized insurance regulatory scheme.

We should further note that preemption questions can be both politically and substantively difficult, as Mr. Muckenfuss and I know from firsthand experience in the context of H.R. 10. The length and detail of Section 104 of H.R. 10 reflects the complexity and difficulty of trying to work through preemption questions. While that section is certainly not the final answer, the work done on H.R. 10 provides a starting point.

Interstate Operation. The question of interstate insurance operations needs to be addressed. We take it as a given that a federal company charter would allow full interstate activity and that a national agent license would do likewise. (Although the focus of this program is on company chartering, there are many reasons to address sales and distribution as well.) With nationwide activity should come seamlessness of regulation, both at the company level and at the agent level.

Nationwide insurance business through a single charter is a principal reason for creating a federal charter and would represent a fundamental change from the current system. While there would be individual winners and losers among companies and agents, the experience in the banking industry strongly suggests that it is not inconsistent with a dual federal-state system or with strong competition among entities of all sizes. The advent of interstate banking has not killed the state banking system, but rather has challenged it to adapt to a new environment—a challenge that the state bank system has successfully met.

How the Conference of State Bank Supervisors (CSBS) dealt with the advent of interstate banking is instructive. Soon after the interstate bill was passed, CSBS set about to create a system of regulation for state banks comparable to what national banks have under the single Comptroller of the Currency. The result was a cooperative framework in which the state regulators allocate and share revenues and responsibilities for examination and supervision.

That initial work proved insufficient, and in 1996, the CSBS took up an amendment long sought by state banks and made it the top CSBS legislative priority. CSBS succeeded in getting an amendment to the interstate banking law to confirm that the law of a state bank's home state will follow that bank as it establishes interstate operations. The states now have a system that preserves state banking regulation while allowing state banks to have competitive interstate branches. Nevertheless, the inherent advantages of national banks have only been minimized, not eliminated.

During that period, the state bank regulators had to address the question of state sovereignty and their prerogative to rule their fiefdoms without regard to what federal or other state regulators might do. They have had to adapt in the interstate environment, but they have done it in a way that really preserves the essence of what they care about in the state system, and it has been a positive change for the state bank system.

A federal insurance charter will raise similar challenges for the regulation of those companies that remain state chartered and operate interstate. Indeed, the states should want to create a framework that will make it attractive to remain state chartered. Bank regulators have responded creatively to that challenge, and there is every reason to believe the insurance commissioners would do so as well.

Before moving to the next topic, a word about e-commerce is in order. E-commerce raises questions that are simply a variant on the interstate banking issue from a legal perspective. E-commerce certainly intensifies the question, because it transcends geography by permitting transactions to take place by electronic means involving a potentially unlimited number of providers (as well as buyers) in an unlimited number of places around the world. It fundamentally calls into question jurisdiction segmented by geography.

Federal Agency Structure. A fourth question, which has been touched on by a number of speakers, is agency structure: what type of regulatory structure would there be, and where would it be located within the federal government? A conceptually distinct issue is whether there is a federal guaranty fund, and if so, what is its structure and location on the federal agency map. Chartering and guaranty functions do not necessarily have to be in the same agency.

The dual banking system evolved over time. After President Andrew Jackson vetoed the renewal of the charter of the Second Bank of the United States in the 1830s, there were only state banks. In the 1860s, to help finance the Civil War, the National Bank Act was passed. During the 1930s, when federal deposit insurance was adopted, the Federal Deposit Insurance Corporation (FDIC) was created as a separate agency. On the thrift side, there was originally a close connection between the deposit insurance fund and the federal charter regulator, which were controlled by the same three-member board. The S&L debacle of the 1980s led to a rethinking of that arrangement. Now the FDIC provides deposit insurance for both thrifts and banks through two separate funds. The Office of the Comptroller of the Currency

(OCC) and the OTS remain separate units within the Treasury Department. (Proposals to merge the OCC and the OTS so far have not taken off politically.)

The next question concerns the structure of the agency: a single-headed agency, or a multimember board? Available models are the OCC or the OTS, single-headed bureaus under the Treasury Department, versus the FDIC or the Fed, which have multimember boards and are independent agencies. If you locate it in a department, which department do you choose?

Further, should any self-regulatory organization be built into the structure, as is done with securities regulation? Each of those questions involves any number of significant considerations.

In view of the various opinions already expressed by other contributors to this volume, we suggest that the OCC is the model that ought to be seriously considered. Although a bureau within the Treasury Department, the OCC has had a history of independence. Because Treasury is one of the major cabinet departments and typically has a powerful secretary within the executive branch, a bureau within that department potentially has greater clout than it would have as an independent agency. Moreover, because tax policy is important, an insurance industry with an insurance administrator or regulator located in the same department that does tax policy may have some advantages. In sum, the OCC has been an effective advocate for the banking agenda within the federal government without giving up on its role as a tough regulator.

The existence of the powerful and independent Federal Reserve certainly makes it potentially attractive as either a model for an independent federal insurance regulatory agency or an agency to house a new insurance regulatory function. The Fed is indeed a very powerful actor in Washington, but it is unique because of its primary role as the central bank and manager of monetary policy. Bank regulation today is a secondary function at the Fed, and it is not clear how the addition of an insurance regulatory mission would fit into that agency's structure. The secondary importance of the regulatory function today tends to magnify the clout of Fed staff, which has even less public accountability than have the Fed governors. The Fed model or option seems problematic.

Additional issues also deserve attention, although I will only sketch them out here:

Enforcement authority. The banking model regarding enforcement should be carefully considered, but it may not be apt. Indeed, in the wake of the S&L debacle of the 1980s, the penalties for violation of the federal banking laws were drastically increased and reach those who advise or provide services to insured depositories. Some commentators have suggested that the penalties for violating banking laws are greater than those for being a drug dealer.

Charter qualification and entry controls. There is, obviously, a need for entry qualifications to establish or acquire control of a federal insurance company.

Conversion issues. Among the transition issues to be addressed are those involving conversion from a state to a federal charter. Because of the many mutual insurance companies that exist today, another necessary question is whether there will be a federal mutual charter and what rules will govern conversion from mutual to stock. The OTS and FDIC have extensive experience with mutual-to-stock conversion issues, but because a mutual insurance policyholder may have economic interests in the company's surplus that a bank depositor does not have in a mutual bank, the demutualization of insurers involves substantively different considerations.

Holding company issues. Most of the states have adopted the model insurance holding company act. In addition, some insurers are already subject to OTS holding company supervision because they control a thrift. The pending financial modernization bills, H.R. 10 and S. 900, would make the insurers or insurance holding companies that control an insured bank subject to Fed "umbrella" supervision. Against that backdrop, the first question we ought to ask is whether a new federal insurance charter need bring any kind of holding company regulation. Affiliate transaction protections can be adopted instead of holding company regulation.

Consumer protection, antidiscrimination, and community investment. Over the years, banks have been made subject to a significant number of laws advancing consumer protection and social objectives such as antidiscrimination and community reinvestment. Insurers that engage in consumer or mortgage lending are already subject to some of those laws. Such issues have been raised in the consideration of H.R. 10 and S. 900, and they would surely be raised in the consideration of a federal insurance charter bill.

Subsidiary activities. A number of insurer clients have bought banks under the company's investment authority. The question of subsidiary activities as such was not itself a major issue, except when the state had an anti-affiliation statute. The impulse behind those statutes has surfaced in the national bank context. The whole question of operating subsidiary ("op-sub") activities in insurance sales and underwriting continues to be a significant question in H.R. 10, and a zero-base approach to that issue seems particularly appropriate.

State guaranty funds. Finally, there is the question of the state guaranty funds, which has been adequately covered by others in this monograph.

Remarks by Cantwell F. Muckenfuss III

The evolution of a national marketplace—indeed, a global marketplace—cries out for a truly national alternative. Put simply, the absence of a national alternative that is uniform and seamless for significant national insurance operations, at best, adds cost and time to the development and provision of insurance products to the consumer. Furthermore, the effort to address those questions systematically will have concrete benefits. A thoroughgoing substantive review of insurance regulation will highlight areas where improvements need to take place.

Before amplifying those points, I should note that I have been struck by the tepid support for a federal option from among the contributors to this volume (apart from those tasked with making a pro or con argument). It is quite natural that state insurance regulators do not support the idea of a new federal regulatory framework. Although I am confident that state insurance regulators would survive and flourish, a federal alternative would undoubtedly encroach and diminish revenues and personnel. Similarly, it is natural that trade associations and companies are careful in their criticism of the regulators they must live with day to day. I expected, however, far greater enthusiasm from the academic community. For proponents of the free market and the benefits of competition, the case for a federal regulatory alternative should be overwhelming and, in fact, for many years it has been overwhelming.

First, and most obviously, we now have a truly national market for financial services. What has always made sense has been made irresistible by the drive of technology. The absence of uniform products and rules and the multiplicity of licensing and filing requirements inevitably add cost and burden to both providers and consumers. That factor is exacerbated by the proliferation of hybrid products combining elements of securities, banking, and insurance. That phenomenon will *only* increase as the Internet and other technologies drive the marketplace.

Second, despite the best efforts of the NAIC, quality and responsiveness are not uniform among the states. It is certainly no secret that timeliness is a problem in some states. Theory suggests, and my own experience confirms, that a little healthy competition among regulators almost always improves performance. Here again, choice would promote efficiency and improve competition and would benefit both providers and consumers.

Third, theory also suggests—and my experience as a practicing lawyer and as a regulator at *two* federal agencies that, in reality, do compete—confirms strongly the proposition that competitive choices promote innovation. In the banking arena, recent history is replete with examples. Without belaboring the point, there is no doubt that healthy competition between the Fed and OCC has permitted innovation in the marketplace. "Wild card" statutes enacted at the state level (which allow state banks to engage in all national bank activities without an explicit and specific state authorization) further illustrate the point. And, of course, the prominence of state-chartered banks in New York and the vitality of the state banking system across the country five years after national banks gained interstate branching authority demonstrate that states can effectively provide a competitive alternative.

A national charter will necessarily deregulate geography by allowing nationwide delivery of insurance products from a single bank platform. It should also deregulate product and pricing in a regulatory framework that provides effective protections to policyholders. A federal option should do no less.

Fourth, while more intangible, I believe the industry would benefit from the presence of an agency with in-depth industry knowledge within the federal government. Certainly, the integration of financial organizations and financial products and globalization of *all* financial markets enhance the desirability, if not necessity, of having a federal agency expert in, if not an advocate of, the business of insurance. In a time of economic difficulty or crisis, a federal insurance agency may be a critical player.

In this regard, I know that it is conventional wisdom that reform of the financial regulatory structure does not occur absent crisis or overwhelming problems that cannot be ignored. Perhaps the passage of financial modernization legislation in the coming months, if it occurs, will put that concern to rest. Moreover, financial reform takes time. Even if a perceived crisis proves politically necessary, there is real benefit to developing concrete answers to the questions that must be answered in devising an optional federal structure. One cannot finish a race not started, and experience suggests that rigorous and spirited debate and the crafting of concrete answers will have a salutary effect at the state level even before the passage of federal legislation.

Finally, consideration of a new federal regulatory framework provides a unique opportunity. Because of the McCarran-Ferguson Act, the federal government has been excluded from much of insurance regulation. As a consequence, unlike other financial sectors, *there are no legacy systems*. In designing a new federal regulatory framework, we do not have to re-engineer or reform. Rather, we have the opportunity to *create* a new system that not only incorporates the best that exists at the state level, but that is also based on a contemporary appreciation of the power of market solutions and a full understanding of the implications of technology and the innovations that have occurred in the financial markets. As Mr. Eager's discussion of the issues in the first part of this chapter reflects, the *creation* of a new regime necessarily entails answering a myriad of questions. The discussion in this monograph suggests that we have not fully appreciated just how open-ended the answers to those questions can be.

PART SIX
The Views of Other Stakeholders

11
Broker Organizations

Joel Wood
Council of Insurance Agents and Brokers

This association represents large commercial property/ casualty insurance brokerage firms. We have only about 275 member firms, but those firms sell more than 80 percent of commercial property/casualty insurance products in the United States—which is reflective of the convergence, consolidation, and globalization of our industry. There were 90,000 independent property/casualty insurance agencies in 1975; 55,000 in 1985; and around 42,000 today. More impressive, though, is the reality that so few firms now produce such a large proportion of the business.

Generally speaking, we agree that state regulation has allowed for effective enforcement of mandatory auto insurance coverage. Oversight by individual states provides an essential foundation for the risks assumed by insurers. It is also based on the need to protect consumers from discriminatory local business practices such as redlining. In these respects, the states have played a vital role, we think, and will continue to do so in protecting the consumers from deceptive and unfair business practices.

But individual state efforts have proven far less effective when regulating commercial and international insurance transactions. The client on the commercial side is quite different. Corporations have experienced risk managers and others who examine policy terms, have the ability to analyze claims-paying ability, and so forth. As a result, individual state regulation of interstate and international business acts as an impediment within the very markets it seeks to protect.

Where the current system reasonably requires an insurer to

adhere to the regulations of its state of domicile, it also compels the insurer to negotiate the insurance codes of every other state in which it does business. Multiple rate filings and form filings cost both the insurers and the insured millions of dollars. In many cases, the large commercial insurer is compelled to look to the alternative markets, where there is relief from the redundant regulatory processes.

Surplus lines carriers are at a distinct regulatory advantage there, and are thus able to offer more tailored and specialty coverages more efficiently and cheaply. Ironically, under the current system, non-U.S.-based insurers have an advantage over domestic insurers. A foreign-based insurer can receive approval from a port-of-entry state, and other insurance departments rely on that to allow the non-U.S. insurer to conduct business. Meanwhile, the domestic insurer still has to comply with all the rate filings, market conduct examinations, forms, and licensing requirements.

It is striking and sad to note that the separate nations of Europe have done more to create reciprocity in the business of insurance among nations than the United States has among the fifty states.

In the commercial context, the localized regulation that the McCarran-Ferguson Act supports may no longer be beneficial. The duplicative regulatory requirements that are now imposed on insurance agents and brokers specifically trying to do business in more than one state may do nothing more than impose an unnecessary cost on commercial insurers or consumers with insurable risks in multiple jurisdictions.

Our association's work on H.R. 10 has been devoted almost exclusively to the promotion of the National Association of Registered Agents and Brokers (NARAB) multistate licensing provisions of the legislation. Many agents—particularly those selling life insurance and "personal" lines, such as homeowner's and auto insurance—are licensed in only one or two states, so it is not a particular impediment to them. But the current system requires licenses to be obtained on a line-by-line, class-by-class, producer-by-producer, state-by-state basis. Particularly in the commercial/industrial insurance arena, this system usually requires a single agent or broker to hold scores of licenses with all sorts of duplicative and unnecessary requirements that have little or nothing to do with their standards of professionalism. An agent or broker marketing a national insurance program may routinely have to obtain more than one hundred licenses. It is exceptionally difficult for an agency or brokerage doing business in multiple jurisdictions to have all its producers in full compliance with the thousands of individual state licensing requirements.

The most problematic licensing issues are state residency requirements. Several states require agents or brokers to incorporate their agency inside the state in which they are soliciting business. Still other states do not allow nonresident brokers to solicit business at all. In an era when the volume of interstate insurance sales is exponentially increasing, requirements surrounding state residency are a significant barrier to interstate commerce. They also create costs that are passed on to consumers.

Here is what the NARAB provisions of H.R. 10 would do. First, the subtitle allows states two mechanisms to avert the creation of NARAB. If a majority of states enact uniform licensing or reciprocity laws within three years of the enactment of the subtitle, NARAB will not come into existence. If a majority of states have not met the criteria of uniformity or reciprocity, the National Association of Insurance Commissioners will then be authorized to establish NARAB. Only if the NAIC does not establish NARAB within two more years (or if it later becomes unable to oversee NARAB for any reason) would NARAB be created as an independent agency. Even during the second two-year "grace period," NARAB would not be formed if a majority of the states representing at least 50 percent of the total U.S. commercial-lines premiums satisfied either the uniformity or reciprocity requirement. In other words, the provision provides the states with at least five years to address multistate licensing issues before NARAB would be created.

If the states do not take action and NARAB is created, the organization itself will not provide a federal license for insurance sales, but rather will serve as a clearinghouse for multistate licensing, so that services may be more efficiently provided to policyholders. NARAB will be charged with imposing licensing and professional qualification requirements that exceed the standards of any current state law. It will have the authority to reduce duplicative regulatory requirements that are now imposed on agents and brokers whose clients' needs require them to be licensed to do business in more than one state.

Membership in NARAB will be purely voluntary and self-funding, and it will be open to all state-licensed insurance producers. Membership in NARAB will not eliminate the need for an insurance producer to be licensed in each state in which it sells insurance. Nor will it deprive the states of the revenues they raise through the licensing process. However, NARAB will eliminate needless duplication and create uniformity in the multistate sale of insurance. All state laws and regulations pertaining to insurance producers will remain in force and effect unless they are expressly preempted. The extent of express preemption is extremely limited to residency requirements and other areas of unproductive duplication. State unfair trade practices acts, and all other areas of state law, will remain in effect—including the ability of a state to revoke a license of a NARAB member for cause.

We believe that it is extremely hypocritical for the United States to argue to our trading partners that they should lower their barriers for our insurance industry to compete, while we have outright bans on solicitation in many states, and have all kinds of barriers to interstate competition. NARAB is designed to alleviate that problem. One of the biggest unspoken concerns among our members is a lack of full compliance that occurs amid the morass of thousands and thousands of regulations affecting full interstate agent-broker licensing.

Mr. Hunter's remarks in this monograph note his continuing concern that if insurers want a change in regulatory arrangements, that is probably because they sense a chance to have less regulation, or less competition, or both. Generally, I agree. I wish I could do more about limiting competition for our members. I tried that routine for years, as we agents tried to keep banks out of the business. As for trying to create less regulation, I plead absolutely guilty in the NARAB context—because, as I noted, the hassles associated with licensing have little or nothing to do with standards of professionalism.

In 1939, our association formed its first task force to urge state insurance commissioners to create uniformity in agent-broker licensing standards. In 1991, when Chairman John Dingell had a hearing on the licensing issue, the only witness then representing the NAIC viewpoint said that federal action was unnecessary because within five years, the NAIC's Producer Information Network would result in full-fledged reciprocal and uniform state-by-state licensing practices. Obviously, that goal is woefully short of being met.

In 1997, the NAIC embarked on a uniform treatment model standard—an excellent agenda, wherein states are encouraged to treat residents and nonresidents alike in licensing. Many states have signed on to that model. The problem is that fifty states could sign on but still have fifty separate sets of standards, including standards that could be discriminatory.

Our overarching concern is that the pace of consolidations, the pace of the integration of the financial services industry, and the pace of globalization have far outstripped the pace of reform. That is not primarily the fault of regulators. The industry must look in the mirror to understand how, for example, Florida continues to tolerate a countersignature requirement that forces 50 percent of all commission and fee income to be shared with resident Florida agents when a policy is procured by a nonresident. It has been the goal and practice of local agents and small companies to protect themselves from outside competition.

Finally, I would endorse Mr. Hunter's call for greater congressional scrutiny. The mere act of scrutiny on the solvency issue had a tremendous positive effect within the NAIC in the early 1990s. The presence of NARAB in H.R. 10 during the past two years has galvanized the states to move toward greater uniformity on the licensing front.

The broader question is whether the McCarran-Ferguson Act remains either relevant or necessary in a world where the financial services industry in general (and the insurance industry in particular) has become national in scope, or where World Trade Organization agreements are on the verge of creating fully developed global markets. It has become increasingly apparent, from our perspective, that the policy objectives embodied in the McCarran-Ferguson Act are questionable in the context of an increasingly internationalized insurance world. The duplicative state insurance regulatory requirements to which our national and international members, as well as commercial insurers, are subject under McCarran do not protect the commercial *con-*

sumers of those products. McCarran thus serves no functional purpose beyond adding millions of dollars in unnecessary administrative costs. The world has changed since the McCarran-Ferguson Act was initially enacted in 1945, and the time is long past due for seriously considering the manner in which McCarran should be updated to reflect those changes.

When the McCarran-Ferguson Act was enacted in 1945, the business of insurance was predominantly local in character, regardless of the type of insurance being sold. On the commercial side, the insurable risks of most businesses were localized—although interstate commerce in the form of the transport and sale of goods was already well developed.

The business of insurance has obviously changed over the course of the intervening decades. Many businesses are now exposed to insurable risks in multiple states and countries. Most of the members of the Council are licensed to act as insurance producers in all fifty states. A 1985 letter decision of the Comptroller of the Currency exemplifies the change. In that letter, the Comptroller found that Section 92 of the National Bank Act permits national banks located in small communities to sell insurance not only to customers located in neighboring cities but also to customers located *anywhere,* without any geographic limitation at all. The letter reflects that marketplace realities such as cars, airplanes, telephones, fax machines, and the Internet, among others, have made the longest physical distances spannable (sometimes in microseconds). Insurers and insurance producers now serve customers nationwide and even worldwide, which gives them the power to address the specialized needs that have developed in the increasingly complex and interdependent international marketplace.

As Congress has come to recognize, many components of the policies on which McCarran was grounded have lost their relevance in today's nationalized and internationalized marketplace. That recognition has led to the enactment of laws that directly regulate the business of insurance and preempt conflicting state statutes, including laws that:

- regulate the provision of title insurance;
- require certain insurance-related disclosures;
- authorize the creation of risk-retention groups, even in states that would otherwise prohibit such groups;

- establish mandatory federal requirements for the provision of employee health-care insurance;
- establish mandatory federal requirements for group health plans;
- make certain acts committed by "persons engaged in the business of insurance" crimes under federal law.

In addition, the businesses of the various providers of financial services have become conflated:

- Banks sell insurance and own securities brokerage houses.
- Stockbrokers make loans and sell insurance.
- Insurance companies own banks and brokerage houses.

Those providers are located all over the world, and they are offering an increasingly complex array of specialized products. In many instances, they have the benefit of being subject to a unitary regulator for the bulk of their activities.

Hence, state regulation of the insurance business, although still "relevant," may no longer be beneficial for the commercial side of our business. Perhaps the best evidence of that fact is the position of the leading voice for the consumers of commercial insurance—the Risk and Insurance Management Society (RIMS), an association whose membership includes more than 8,000 professional risk managers and more than 4,500 corporations, representing the largest group of commercial insurance consumers in the world. RIMS historically opposed all efforts to reform or repeal McCarran, but in 1993 it changed its position and now favors federal regulation of large commercial insurers and brokers because of the large cost savings it believes would be fostered by such a change.

To conclude, the business of insurance and the risks that the participants in that business seek to insure have changed since the enactment of the McCarran-Ferguson Act. Especially in the commercial context, the insurance business is simply no longer a local one. It is national and international in scope and character, as are the businesses of those who seek insurance protection. McCarran and the quilt of state-based regulation it supports stand as an obstacle to the efficient servicing of this commercial insurance business.

Thus, we think that a purely optional federal charter makes sense, such as proposed by the American Bankers Association, particularly for commercial lines.

12

Insurance Agents and Advisers

Michael Kerley
National Association of Life Underwriters

I t is extraordinary and valuable to take an in-depth review of what we virtually take for granted in our industry—state regulation of insurance.

We insurance agents have traditionally come down on the side of preferring state regulation of insurance. We defend the current system. Maybe that is because for the most part our membership is made up of life and health insurance agents, as opposed to property/casualty insurance agents. I do not sense that life agents have as many licensing difficulties in the states as some of our property/casualty brethren do.

Certainly, though, many in our association membership act as agents for what we call multiline insurance companies, such as Allstate and State Farm. And, of course, those people are obviously in the property/casualty insurance business as well. But I do not hear a lot of complaints from the vast majority of our members about some of the practical difficulties that, for example, Mr. Wood has addressed.

You can say this about our industry: at the end of this day, you really have to wonder where in the world we are going.

I know where we have been. Our association is 109 years old. That means that people have been passing down oral history for 109 years. Some of it is recorded, and some of it is not recorded. They talk about things like the Armstrong investigation, back in 1905. It gets you to thinking about what regulation is all about. "Do we need regulation?" is the very first question anybody ought to ask himself.

What are the purposes of regulation? From an industry

standpoint, of course, the first purpose of regulation is to make sure that the industry has a good reputation.

Agents tend to think of regulation as protecting the image of the industry, protecting the image of agents, and providing an opportunity for the people that we all claim we are here for—consumers—to have their voices heard. Most agents would agree that the state regulatory system has, by and large, done a pretty good job, and by and large, we would like to keep it the way it is.

I assumed I would know where all the parties contributing to this volume would stand on the issue, and I thought the majority of the contributors would come down on the side of federal regulation as a substitute for state regulation. I am particularly taken aback by comments from some of the academics to the effect that the case is not that strong. We agents do not have to examine this issue at length; we think that state regulation does the things that we want it to do.

The bigger the company, the more likely it is that it will want national regulation. An international company wants international regulation. For a property/casualty agency that is national in scope or for a large national group, having one national regulator may be the solution of choice. But for an average agent—and a lot of our people are not average, as they do business in many, many states and have some of the same problems that Mr. Wood has described—the thinking is often that regulation closest to the people is the best.

Our people, the agents, are in the field with consumers every day. Other organizations take polls, but our members actually are sitting across tables, talking to people who buy insurance. And most of them seem to think that having local contacts is a good thing.

So we thought about it, and looked at various federal regulatory schemes. We have looked at the obvious ones, for banking and securities, and looked at the Food and Drug Administration, and we conclude, "Well, there's some good, there's some bad." We have, in effect, fifty regulators. To some extent that is good, because it means that power is diversified.

Many of our members would like to have one license to do business across state lines, just like insurance companies. They would like to have one place to register and be able to do business in all of the fifty states.

But we believe that state regulation will improve in part because of programs like this. Every time there is movement in the federal government to step in and do something, it seems to spur the NAIC, and state insurance commissioners in general, to go forward. I see us in that kind of period right now.

Those of us contributing to this volume who speak about reductions in the regulatory level are more heartened now than we have been for a long while. Our members do not like rate regulation, although life insurance is one of the lines of business that is least likely to be regulated. But a lot of regular life insurance agents also sell property/casualty insurance and health insurance.

Those in the health insurance arena are particularly mindful of the complications that state-mandated benefits bring to the sales equation. Because while many of them are doing business only in a local arena, many others are doing business in multiple states. When you travel from state to state and you encounter the multiple mandated requirements, it does tend to be vexing.

But I am somewhat optimistic at this moment that the industry will help the NAIC to come to grips with many of those issues.

13

A Consumer Perspective

J. Robert Hunter
Consumer Federation of America

Overview

The question we are considering in this volume is whether there should be a change in how insurance is regulated. Specifically, should there be federal charters as an option for insurers?

Consumers believe there is good reason for this question at this moment in the development of insurance in America, but we believe the nation lacks the information to determine just what needs to be done. Thus, Congress should undertake a one-year study of insurance regulation to determine what it should look like in the twenty-first century.

Congress should study this question from all perspectives, including those of insurers, agents, banks and other real and potential competitors of insurance, state regulators, potential federal regulators, and, most important, the business and personal consumers. Some of the issues that should be addressed from the consumer perspective are:

- What functions are necessary to obtain effective insurance regulation from the consumer viewpoint?
- How well has the current state insurance regulatory system served consumers?
- Are systematic changes underway in the insurance market that might affect the status quo and make a new approach to regulation preferable for consumers?
- What should the roles of the states and the federal government be, with respect to the regulation of insurance?

Before I address those questions, I want to stress the point that Congress needs to undertake an in-depth study to understand what must be done and by whom in an effective insurance regulatory system for the new century.

History

The question of where regulation should occur has been debated before in this country. Every few decades, insurance companies wonder if the grass is a bit greener in the federal system than under state regulation. In the past century, when the federal government had a laissez-faire approach and states were beginning to create insurance departments, the industry decided to move to federal control. In a Supreme Court decision in *Paul v. Virginia*, the Court held that insurance was not interstate commerce and thus not subject to federal control. Thus, the insurance companies lost in their attempt to obtain easier regulation.

The insurers were soon happy to have lost that case, when the trustbusters came to Washington. But the insurance cartel's anticompetitive practices became so egregious that the Court revisited the question. This time the insurers were on the side of continuing the less vigorous state system. But, in the 1944 *South-Eastern Underwriters* case, the Court reversed itself and ruled that insurance was interstate commerce and subject to federal regulation. The insurance companies just could not seem to win in court.

However, the losing streak was short lived. The industry lobbied hard to get the *South-Eastern Underwriters* decision reversed legislatively. A year after the decision, Congress passed the McCarran-Ferguson Act, which delegated the regulation of insurance back to the states with no oversight or minimum standards for acceptable regulatory effort. That was a big insurer victory.

But that was not all that the insurers won. Each house of Congress passed the bill with a two-year moratorium on antitrust enforcement, which should have meant an end to anticompetitive activities such as rate bureaus as early as 1947. However, in conference, some industry lobbyist really earned his salary by sliding in a permanent moratorium, which still diminishes insurance competition today, more than half a century later. Even President Franklin Roosevelt did not understand that as he signed the bill into law.[1]

Consumers, including such business consumers as nurses and retail druggists, have unsuccessfully fought for reversal or amendment of the antitrust exemption.

Consumers can draw four conclusions from this history:

- If insurers want a change in regulatory arrangements, that is probably because they sense a chance to have less regulation, or less competition, or both.
- Consumers had better look with great caution at any industry attempt to change the current regulatory arrangement.
- Unlike President Roosevelt's staff, we ought to pay attention during the end game as the bill goes through Congress.
- We should not hold any illusions that either arena of government—state or federal—is inherently the best for consumers.

Now let us take a look at the key questions Congress should address from a consumer perspective:

Question 1—What Functions Are Required to Obtain Effective Insurance Regulation?

Several functions should be performed to regulate insurance effectively. All are consumer protections. They are:

- *Solvency regulation.* It does a consumer no good to pay in premiums for decades, only to have an insurance product fail when an insured event occurs.
- *Consumer education.* Insurance is a difficult product to understand. Price, service, and solvency information must be made available if private vendors do not do so. Flow of information to private vendors should be ensured.
- *Competitive information.* Regulation should assist in making information available to smaller insurers and new entrants so that their actuarial needs can be met and competition can be enhanced.
- *Law enforcement.* The insurance regulator must enforce the insurance code in many aspects, sometimes with the cooperation of traditional law enforcement, sometimes without that help (such as in civil fines).

- *Licensing*. The regulator ensures the public that executives who run agents and companies are not incompetents or felons.
- *Market review*. The regulator monitors the market for failures in competition to address critical shortages or potential anticompetitive practices.
- *Ratemaking*. The regulator monitors prices in some way, either directly or through monitoring the competitiveness of the insurance market.

Question 2—Has State Regulation Served to Protect Consumers?

Let me try to answer this question by first saying something that may not surprise anyone, and saying another thing that may surprise a few.

The nonsurprising thing is that consumers do not care who regulates insurance. Having served as both a federal employee (federal insurance administrator) and a state employee (Texas insurance commissioner), I can assure you that either arena of government has the ability, about equally, to mess up or achieve any job you give it.

What consumers do care about is the effectiveness of regulation.

The potentially surprising thing I have to say is that the Consumer Federation of America (CFA) does not favor effective regulation over effective competition. From a philosophical viewpoint, as well as from a viewpoint hammered into us by years of failed state efforts, we prefer competition.[2] Now, the level of trust in competition varies in a few important ways. First, there is a general income level component in people's trust of competition. Poorer, less educated consumers do not trust large institutions, and with good reason. For instance, from my experience and from analysis of zip code data, redlining has been practiced by at least some insurers.[3]

A second concern with competition is that there are some insurance products, such as credit insurance, where the selector of the insurance company gets a commission and the payer is a third party. That arrangement leads to "reverse competition," where the cost of insurance is high to allow a noncompetitive commission. Rates must be regulated in that and other noncompetitive situations.

Finally, competition in personal and small business lines of insurance is currently hampered by the federal antitrust law exemption as well as by state laws that diminish competitive forces.

I should add that consumers define "competition" classically, not as the insurance companies often do. For example, we do not believe that competition can be effective if "competitors" can agree on prices or even on such elements of pricing as the anticipated cost changes over the coming year.[4] In other words, we think that competition requires antitrust laws to be applied to insurance as they are to the rest of American business. We also believe that those laws that grant insurers resale price maintenance over agents should be struck down. So should laws that prohibit groups from forming to purchase insurance.

CFA was one of the first groups, besides banks themselves, to support bank entry into insurance, over insurer and agent opposition. We do not like entry barriers, except for crooks or inept managers. We do seek state action to make insurance price information available in computer readable format, so that private information systems can be developed to help consumers find the best insurance prices. We think the twenty-first century will see the rise of information brokers and the decline, and perhaps extinction, of agency-type arrangements (insurance agents, travel agents, and so forth).[5] We look forward to those developments and believe that regulation can help get the information flowing electronically to the private information brokers who are emerging.

With the above as background, how well have the states been handling the regulation of insurance companies?

States have been free to do whatever they want as they regulate insurance.[6] The federal interest has been almost nonexistent. There are few reviews of state regulation by Congress, the latest occurring twenty years ago, when the General Accounting Office (GAO) looked at state regulation.

In its 1979 report entitled "Issues and Needed Improvements in State Regulation of the Insurance Business," the GAO was sharply critical of lax consumer protections and of elements that diminished competition, such as inadequate consumer information.

The Consumer Federation of America has recently issued three reports on the quality of consumer information available from the states twenty years after the GAO critique. The states have modestly upgraded their information. But consider this: twenty-two states have no price information on auto or health insurance; thirty states do not have homeowner's information; no state has life insurance price data. As to service information, twenty-nine states have no information on complaints for auto insurance, thirty-five do not have it for homeowner's insurance, thirty-nine do not have it for life insurance, and thirty-six do not have it for health insurance. State web page information is quite good, but many states have no price or service information online.

CFA believes that the states do too little to ensure that full competitive forces are at play in insurance. Few monitor the market at all. They are surprised when a liability crisis occurs. They did not make sure that small regional insurance companies had reinsurance before the hurricanes struck.

The General Accounting Office criticized state regulation as being "too cozy" with those being regulated. There was a revolving door in regulation—half of the commissioners came from and half went to the industry.

Our research shows that that ratio has remained steady over the past twenty years. Worse, our research shows that state insurance legislators on the committees dealing with insurance are, about one-fifth of the time, employed by the industry.

There was a period when state regulation tried to improve itself. The late 1980s and early 1990s saw a trend toward more independence from industry control. Even the National Association of Insurance Commissioners (NAIC) was starting to exert some influence on establishing minimum national criteria for solvency regulation.

But the insurance companies did not tolerate that. Threatening the NAIC with a cutoff of funds, they forced the NAIC to cave in to industry demands and back off.

The NAIC and all of state regulation has been in retreat ever since.

A classic example of ineptitude is the collapse of confidence in life insurance in the wake of the Prudential, Met Life, and New York Life sales abuses. The states' failure to protect consumers inevitably led to the impossible statement (can we actually utter this?), "Thank God for the trial lawyers." After New Jersey went after Prudential and slapped its wrist, should it be surprising that it was later revealed that the New Jersey involvement came at the request of Prudential?

Then there are the periodic crises:

- insurance insolvencies of the late 1980s;
- liability crises in the mid-1970s and mid-1980s;
- auto rates out of control in a so-called "competitive" state, with rate collusion leading to the enactment of Proposition 103 in California.

State regulation has, in my view, not been effective for consumers of insurance. Any congressional study should document the weaknesses of state regulation from consumer and other viewpoints, so that repair, either through federal or state action, can be made. The study should look at each key area listed above to determine if the states are doing an adequate job. Here is a consumer view on each of those areas:

Solvency regulation. The states have not had a meltdown such as the S&L crisis, but they have not been sterling regulators either. In its review of the role of states in this area, Congress issued "Failed Promises," which was sharply critical of how the states undertook this aspect of regulation. The states did adopt the NAIC accreditation program to set national standards for regulation solvency, but that was softened by industry pressure once John Dingell was no longer chair of the Commerce Committee. The state guaranty funds, with no funding, are not likely to work well if a crisis occurs.

Consumer education. States have done a fair job of getting information into the hands of consumers or information brokers. Much more must be done, as recent CFA reports have documented.

Competitive information. Regulators have been too quick to adopt an insurer's claim that information is a trade secret. The large insurers are doing all they can to bottle up information the market needs to perform efficiently. That has been a deteriorating situation that requires action.

Law enforcement. The insurance departments are weak in this area. A classic example is the awful handling of the Prudential market conduct situation discussed above.

Licensing. The states have done a poor job here. As an example, a bad agent in one state has been able to go next door and start up business. The NAIC is creating a national system to address this, however.

Market review. The states have utterly failed in this task. Most state regulators make no attempt to understand the market or to do a full-fledged assessment of the competitiveness of a market. Certainly there is no regulator studying the national trends. That situation is dangerous for the nation's economy, since we could be blind-sided by events because of the lack of monitoring. The states were surprised, for instance, when the liability crises occurred.

Ratemaking. The insurance companies seek deregulation of rates. However, they do not want to have antitrust laws applied, as competitive industries have done. Nor do they want other anticompetitive laws taken off the books. What they really seem to want is deregulated cartel structures. Consumers want a regulator who thinks through this issue and makes a decision to go either to competition or to regulation, and to make *all* the changes necessary to accomplish that. Consumers do not want halfway measures—in between the two approaches. We will slip through the cracks if clarity is not achieved. Unfortunately, almost no states have thought this through, and the insurance companies like the confusion.

Question 3—Are Trends Underway in Insurance That Imply Changes in Regulatory Structure?

Here are a few major economic trends that have insurance regulatory implications:

- *International trade agreements.* These started with NAFTA, but they lead well beyond the Americas. The trend is for more large and complex international players to dominate the insurance market. Those arrangements may prove to be beyond the capacity of some (and perhaps all) states. Certainly, no state can enter into a treaty with another nation if such a treaty is needed to make regulation effective.

- *Merger mania.* Mergers are a way of life in today's world economy. Huge insurance providers are emerging. International purchases and deals to gain U.S. shares are commonplace. Can understaffed states keep up with those giant entities? Can those entities be allowed to fail under the nonfunded state guaranty system in place? CFA thinks not. Governor Christie Todd Whitman's reaction to the media questions relating to the soft deal New Jersey gave Prudential was that the company was a large employer in the state. That is not comforting to those many people in New Jersey and around the nation whom Prudential abused.

- *Financial services walls tumbling down.* Banks now act as insurance agents. Can underwriting be far behind? The very word "Citicorp" should send fear into the hearts of advocates of the status quo. Where does the federal bank regulator's role end and the state regulator's begin?

- *Internet and other electronic wizardry.* Billions of dollars daily cross international borders in milliseconds. Sales of insurance take place on the World Wide Web. What's next? Can Wyoming's insurance department's twenty-four staffers really control that insurance web page coming in from Addis Ababa?

- *A race to the bottom.* Vermont and other states are trying to attract the captive insurance industry. That is fine. But the approach of competing by lax regulation is worrisome. We can see the trend toward lax regulation in CIGNA (and in other inappropriate restructurings), where the company was split into a good company and a bad company, to the detriment of the policyholders in the potentially underfunded, runoff, "bad" company. The recent proposals for optional federal charters (optional to insurers, *not* to consumers) could result in this competition in laxity.

Question 4—What Should the Federal Role in Insurance Regulation Be?

The simple answer is, "Not complaint-handling." The more complex answer is, "We're not sure yet."

Since we are not sure yet, Congress should look into those questions of who should regulate. Should there be minimum standards for states to meet? Should Congress take over certain aspects of regulation? Which ones? How do we ensure that there is not a perverse competition for market share through lax regulation between states and the federal government, as there is between some states right now? Should the antitrust exemption be maintained? Could certain efficiencies in money and time be achieved by centralizing certain functions?

Congress also has to consider the federal history with respect to insurance regulation, which can be summed up in three words: "What, me worry?" The federal government's total lack of capacity to understand insurance is troubling. Consider these examples:

- When I testified before Congress during the last liability crisis, I appeared on the same morning as the chairman of the Federal Trade Commission (FTC). He had no prepared statement. When he was asked to explain what the FTC thought was causing the crisis, he answered that he did not know, and if he did know, he would be breaking the law. That was because Congress had taken away the FTC's right to study insurance in 1980. It seems that the FTC had been punished for having had the audacity to tell consumers that whole life insurance was not a good deal. That should give pause to those who think that a federal role would automatically be better.

- The Supreme Court has ruled that ERISA preempts state insurance regulation. That ruling has created a regulatory black hole, wherein consumers can fall to their financial death. As bad as state regulation has been, it has never allowed an insurer to change the rules after a claim occurs. Yet the United States Supreme Court allowed an insurer to lower AIDS coverage from $1 million to $5,000 after a man became ill with the disease.

Conclusion

As Congress reconsiders the possibility of some federal role in insurance, it should not fall into the "either/or" trap that some might set. The federal role might be an optional one, a partial one, minimum standards, technical assistance, or some other new approach. Although my view is that the federal government should not replace all state regulation, since there are at least some things that the states can do better (for example, answering complaints and supplying consumer information), even that should be studied.

It seems to me that state regulators and federal lawmakers could do great things together if they could look beyond the turf issue to the needs of consumers in the coming century. I am certain that the states could use federal help in some areas, but the fear of a federal takeover, of "the camel's nose," blinds the states from taking advantage of those potentials.

It is time for the federal government at least to understand insurance and how it is regulated. Given the megatrends mentioned above and the signs of strain in state regulation, the federal government has a duty to review the delegation embodied in the McCarran-Ferguson Act, to determine if some assistance is required for the states. We need a definition of roles, state and federal, to ensure effective insurance regulation in the twenty-first century.

Notes

1. Other examples abound. The ERISA preemption of state health insurance regulation has been a disaster for consumers. The S&L crisis is another example.

2. See, for example, "A Matter of Policy: How a State Becomes Popular with Insurers—But Not Consumers," *Wall Street Journal* (January 14, 1998): 1.

3. For example, Nationwide Mutual Insurance Company was recently found guilty of redlining by a Richmond, Virginia, jury. The fine was more than $100 million. On appeal, the case settled for $17.5 million, and it changed the manner in which business is done nationally.

4. Those are the so-called trend factors.

5. In "commodity" insurance lines, such as the personal lines and small business lines of insurance, direct sales tools are sharply reducing the market share of traditional agents. That is not unique to insurance. Travel agents are being squeezed by direct sales approaches as well.

6. With modest exception (for example, of ERISA, or of flood insurance), the federal government has avoided insurance.

14

The Banking Industry

Larry LaRocco
ABA Insurance Association

The organization that I represent, the American Bankers Association Insurance Association (ABAIA), has been working on a proposal for some time, and I am delighted to share some thoughts about it. The ABAIA is a separately chartered and incorporated subsidiary of the ABA, the American Bankers Association. Today we have fourteen members, all of which are actively engaged in the sale of insurance products and annuities, and most of which underwrite certain lines of insurance, particularly credit insurance. Additionally, several of our members are engaged in underwriting and reinsurance activities outside the United States.

Our members are BANKONE, BankAmerica, BankBoston, Chase, Citigroup, First American, First Security, First Union, JP Morgan, KeyCorp, National City, PNC, Wachovia, and Wells Fargo. They are major players. And with respect to Mr. Muckenfuss's comments about considering the size of organizations just ten years ago, the banks are in this business to stay.

Our mission statement provides that ABAIA is to "serve as a forum for long-term national strategy among banking organizations on insurance matters, [and] to propose legislation and regulations that permit banking organizations to participate fully in the business of insurance." It goes on to state that we "monitor insurance developments at the state level with the support of the nationwide network of state banking associations" and "cooperate with other banking trade associations on issues, programs, and policies of mutual interest." Our top priority recently has been H.R. 10 and the financial modernization bills in

Congress. We have been working on the legislation, and we are still deeply involved in the process.

But another long-term national issue we have identified as a priority is the federal regulation of insurance. We believe that a single federal insurance regulator would simplify regulatory compliance requirements and stimulate the development of uniform products. As many others point out in this volume, banks can be chartered and regulated either by the federal government or by an individual state. That chartering option for banks is commonly called the dual banking system.

The banking industry has operated under that dual system for more than 130 years—since 1863, when the National Bank Act was enacted. The force behind the dual banking system was President Abraham Lincoln. As president, Lincoln proposed and pushed for the passage of the National Bank Act. He did so because he realized that as the economy grew, it needed a system of national banks to complement the then-existing system of state banks. Lincoln, characteristically, was visionary. Today we have two strong, complementary banking systems. Of the approximately 9,000 commercial banks, roughly one-third are nationally chartered and the remaining two-thirds are state chartered.

There are various reasons for a bank to select a national charter over a state charter. One major reason, especially for banks with operations in several states, is to be regulated by a single federal regulator instead of multiple state regulators. Another reason is that national banks are able to offer a more uniform set of products than state banks. We believe that the benefits of the dual banking system can be translated to the insurance industry through the creation of a federal insurance regulatory structure that is similar to the federal regulatory structure for banks.

With that background, I would like to turn to the specifics of our proposal. I should add, however, that our proposal is a work in progress. Although it has been endorsed by ABAIA's Board of Directors, the details are subject to change. It is a blueprint, an outline, a concept. The draft that I have here with me reads, "The Federal Insurance Act of 1998." We have been working on this for more than a year. It has marginal notes because we are changing it all the time.

With that caveat, we as an organization have actually signed off on this proposal. It is something we really believe in, and we hope to push, promote, and work with others to get it enacted. Many of the contributors to this volume have already sat across the table and shared this idea. We have gotten great feedback, and at the right time we hope to be back at the table as a major player.

Federal Insurance Commissioner

Our present proposal calls for the establishment of an Office of the Federal Insurance Commissioner within the Treasury Department. That office would be patterned after two other Treasury bureaus, the Office of the Comptroller of the Currency, which charters and regulates national banks, and the Office of Thrift Supervision, which charters and regulates federal savings and loans. Like those offices, the Office of the Federal Insurance Commissioner would be headed by a single individual, appointed by the president and confirmed by the Senate, for a five-year term.

The obvious alternative structure, which we considered, would be a new, independent federal agency managed by a board, something similar to the Securities and Exchange Commission. There are good arguments for that structure—most notably, its independence. We concluded, however, that it would be better to have a single individual in charge, rather than a board. An individual has the ability to act more quickly and more effectively than a board. Also, we believe that a five-year term provides the individual with an appropriate degree of independence from political pressures.

Powers of the Commissioner

Our proposal gives the commissioner the authority to provide for the "formation, chartering, examination, operation, supervision, and regulation of federal insurance firms." That broad statement of the commissioner's powers is patterned after the statutory powers of the director of the Office of Thrift Supervision by the Home Owners' Loan Act, which is the federal statute governing federally chartered savings and loans. We based the commissioner's powers on that authority because the U.S. Supreme Court has said that, as a general rule, federal savings and loans are subject only to federal law, not state law.

Thus, by patterning the powers of the federal insurance commissioner after the powers of the director of the Office of Thrift Supervision, we hope to ensure that federally chartered insurance firms would be subject to the federal chartering law and the regulations issued by the commissioner.

We did not base the commissioner's powers on the powers granted to the Comptroller of the Currency by the National Bank Act, because the preemptive powers of the Comptroller are not as broad as those given to the director of the Office of Thrift Supervision. The general rule under the National Bank Act is that national banks must comply with state laws, unless those laws interfere with the legitimate activities of the bank. That means that the Comptroller of the Currency must act to preempt certain state laws.

It is just the reverse for the director of the Office of Thrift Supervision. Under the Home Owners' Loan Act, federal thrifts are subject only to those state laws that the director of the Office of Thrift Supervision determines do not interfere with the basic activities of the thrift.

It was our hope that by giving the federal insurance commissioner this so-called cradle-to-grave regulatory power, we would not need to include a separate provision preempting state law. To ensure such treatment, however, it may be necessary to include a separate preemption provision that provides that "no federally chartered insurance firm shall be subject to any state law, regulation, order, interpretation, or other action related to any subject matter addressed in the federal chartering act."

Charters

Our proposal is modeled on the dual banking system. Thus, the federal insurance commissioner would grant federal charters only to those insurance firms that seek them. No one would be compelled to obtain a federal charter. Each insurance firm would be free to select the charter, federal or state, that best suited its needs and the needs of its customers.

Insurance firms could select from two different types of federal charters. The commissioner would be authorized to charter a "federal insurance *association*," which could underwrite, reinsure, broker, or sell insurance products or annuities. Alternatively, the commissioner could charter a "federal insurance *agency*," which could only broker or sell insurance products and annuities.

A federal insurance association and a federal insurance agency could be formed by any person or entity. In other words, those charters could be issued to a single individual, a group of individuals, a corporation, or a partnership, as long as the organizing individual, individuals, or entity satisfied organizational and operational standards established by the commissioner. State-chartered insurance firms would be free to switch to a federal charter, and conversely, a federally chartered insurance firm would be free to switch to a state charter.

A subsidiary of a federal insurance association or a federal insurance agency could engage in any activity permissible for the parent. Also, federally chartered insurance firms could be owned by any company. However, a parent company would be required to provide information to the commissioner on its activities, operations, and financial condition. The commissioner would have the power to force the divestiture of a federal insurance affiliate if the commissioner determined that the affiliate posed a serious risk to the stability of the federal insurance firm. Transactions between a federal insurance association or a federal insurance agency and any affiliate would be required to be fair and reasonable.

Supervisory and Consumer Standards

Under our proposal, the commissioner would be given the authority to establish supervisory and consumer standards to ensure that each federal insurance association or agency operates safely, soundly, and fairly.

The supervisory standards applicable to federal insurance associations—that is, underwriters—would include capital requirements, liquidity requirements, investment and lending requirements, and accounting and valuation requirements. Those, and other requirements, were taken from the solvency bill proposed by Congressman John Dingell in the early 1990s.

The commissioner would be able to take corrective actions

against federally chartered firms that are in a distressed condition. The supervisory standards applicable to federal insurance agencies would focus on bonding, separation of client funds, training, and competency qualifications. Currently, the proposal directs the commissioner to adopt market conduct regulations that address matters such as false advertising, discrimination, claims practice, and tie-in sales. We are considering the creation of a self-regulatory organization to establish and police the market conduct requirements. Some of the people with whom we have met have proposed a National Association of Securities Dealers (NASD)-type organization. We are examining the operations of the NASD to determine how that model might be applied in this context.

Guaranty Funds

Our proposal calls for the establishment of a Federal Insurance Guaranty Corporation that would maintain two separate federal guaranty funds for certain insurance policies written by federal insurance associations.

One guaranty fund would be used to satisfy claims arising from the failure of federal insurance associations that underwrite life and health insurance and annuities. The other guaranty fund would be used to satisfy claims arising from the failure of federal insurance associations that underwrite property and casualty risks.

Currently, the proposal provides that those funds, unlike most state guaranty funds, would be funded by regular assessments. We decided against a post-assessment scheme for two reasons. First, as bankers, ABAIA's members are familiar with the regular assessment scheme imposed by the FDIC. Second, we believe that in times of economic stress, a pre-funded guaranty fund will be in a better position to protect policyholders than will a post-assessment scheme.

The commissioner, who would chair the Federal Insurance Guaranty Corporation, would be required to set the applicable assessment rate for each of the funds. That rate could be based on risk, premium volume, or some other measure.

When it came to setting the type of policies covered by the funds and determining the limits on claims, we decided to follow the NAIC's Model Guaranty Association Acts, as the policies covered by guaranty funds are consumer policies, not commercial policies.

Finally, the proposal calls for the Federal Insurance Guaranty Corporation to act as a conservator or receiver of any federal insurance association that the commissioner determines to be insolvent.

Rates

In a significant departure from current practice, the proposal would prohibit the commissioner from regulating rates. The banking industry has long since abandoned rate regulation, and has found that competition adequately protects the interests of consumers. We assume that that would be the case in the insurance industry.

Furthermore, in an effort to ensure adequate competition, the proposal would not exempt federal insurance associations or federal insurance agencies from federal antitrust laws. And it would require all federally chartered firms to disclose rates and terms to the commissioner.

Fees and Taxes

The only provision in the proposal related to fees is one that permits the commissioner to impose such fees as are necessary to cover the expenses of the Office of the Federal Insurance Commissioner. The proposal does not otherwise change existing state or federal insurance fees or taxes.

Conclusion

In conclusion, ABAIA supports a scheme of federal insurance regulation that is modeled on the existing dual banking system. We believe that such a system would complement the existing system of state regulation. Since it would be voluntary, it would affect only those insurance firms willing to comply with federal regulation.

Who should regulate insurance? With this proposal we can move beyond the "either/or" debate, and answer that the state *and* the federal government should regulate the business. That is a priority for ABAIA.

About the Editor and Authors

PETER J. WALLISON is a resident fellow at the American Enterprise Institute for Public Policy Research, where he co-directs the Program on Financial Market Deregulation. He has served as general counsel of the U.S. Treasury Department, where he played a significant role in the development of the Reagan administration's proposals for deregulation of the financial services industry, and as counsel to President Ronald Reagan. He is the author of *Back from the Brink: A Practical Plan for Privatizing Deposit Insurance and Strengthening Our Banks and Thrifts* (AEI Press, 1991) and the co-author, with Bert Ely, of *Nationalizing Mortgage Risk: The Growth of Fannie Mae and Freddie Mac* (AEI Press, 2000).

JACK CHESSON is senior legislative counsel at the Washington, D.C., office of the National Association of Insurance Commissioners, responsible for handling congressional legislation financial regulation issues.

ROBERT C. EAGER, a partner in the Washington, D.C., office of Gibson, Dunn & Crutcher LLP, focuses on diversified financial services matters.

BERT ELY, the principal at Ely & Company, Inc., is a consultant on financial institutions and monetary policy. He is the co-author, with Peter J. Wallison, of *Nationalizing Mortgage Risk*.

MARTIN F. GRACE is professor of risk management and insurance and legal studies at Georgia State University, and he is the associate director of the Center for Risk Management and Insurance Research.

SCOTT E. HARRINGTON is professor of insurance and finance and Francis M. Hipp Distinguished Faculty Fellow in the Darla Moore School of Business at the University of South Carolina.

J. ROBERT HUNTER is director of insurance for the Consumer Federation of America and a consultant on public policy and actuarial issues.

MICHAEL KERLEY, counsel at the National Association of Life Underwriters, has engaged in all aspects of NALU's government affairs department, with a special emphasis on federal legislation.

ROBERT W. KLEIN is director of the Center for Risk Management and Insurance Research and an associate professor of risk management and insurance at Georgia State University in Atlanta.

LARRY LAROCCO is managing director of the ABA Insurance Association (ABAIA).

ROBERT B. MORGAN is the retired president and chief executive officer of the Cincinnati Financial Corporation (CFC), an insurance holding company located in Cincinnati, Ohio, and of the Cincinnati Insurance Company (CIC), its principal subsidiary.

CANTWELL F. MUCKENFUSS III is a partner in the Washington, D.C., office of Gibson, Dunn & Crutcher LLP, specializing in the representation of financial institutions and coordination of the firm's Financial Institutions Group.

ERNEST T. PATRIKIS is senior vice president and general counsel of the American International Group (AIG).

JACK R. WAHLQUIST is former president and chief executive officer of Lone Star Life Insurance Company of Dallas, Texas.

JOEL WOOD is senior vice president of governmental affairs for the Council of Insurance Agents and Brokers, an association of commercial property and casualty insurance agencies and brokerage firms.

A NOTE ON THE BOOK

This book was edited by Cheryl Weissman
of the publications staff of the
American Enterprise Institute.
The text was set in New Century Schoolbook.
Coghill Composition Company
of Richmond, Virginia, set the type, and
Edwards Brothers of Lillington, North Carolina,
printed and bound the book, using permanent
acid-free paper.

The AEI PRESS is the publisher for the American Enterprise Institute for Public Policy Research, 1150 17th Street, N.W., Washington, D.C. 20036; *Christopher DeMuth,* publisher; *Montgomery Brown,* director; *Ann Petty,* editor; *Leigh Tripoli,* editor; *Cheryl Weissman,* editor; *Kenneth Krattenmaker,* art director and production manager; *Mark Fisher,* senior typesetter; *Jennifer Morretta,* production assistant.

AEI STUDIES ON FINANCIAL MARKET DEREGULATION
Charles W. Calomiris and Peter J. Wallison, series editors

HIGH LOAN-TO-VALUE MORTGAGE LENDING:
PROBLEM OR CURE?
Charles W. Calomiris and Joseph R. Mason

IS THE BANK MERGER WAVE OF THE 1990S EFFICIENT?
LESSONS FROM NINE CASE STUDIES
Charles W. Calomiris and Jason Karceski

NATIONALIZING MORTGAGE RISK:
THE GROWTH OF FANNIE MAE AND FREDDIE MAC
Peter J. Wallison and Bert Ely

OPTIONAL FEDERAL CHARTERING AND
REGULATION OF INSURANCE COMPANIES
Edited by Peter J. Wallison

THE POSTMODERN BANK SAFETY NET:
LESSONS FROM DEVELOPED AND DEVELOPING COUNTRIES
Charles W. Calomiris

REFORMING BANK CAPITAL REGULATION:
A PROPOSAL BY THE U.S. SHADOW FINANCIAL
REGULATORY COMMITTEE
Shadow Financial Regulatory Committee

REGULATING FINANCIAL MARKETS:
A CRITIQUE AND SOME PROPOSALS
George J. Benston